IT'S A Snap!

SECRETS FOR SUCCESSFUL SNAPPING

JEANINE TWIGG

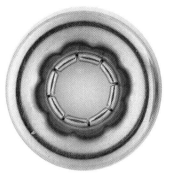

Published by

krause publications

700 East State Street, Iola, WI 54990-0001

The following registered trademark terms and their companies appear in this publication: Gripper® (Scovill Fasteners Inc.), Snapet® (Universal Fasteners Inc.), UltraSuede®, UltraLeather® (Spring Industries), Kwik Sew® (Kwik Sew Pattern Company), The SnapSetter (The Snap Source, Inc.), PolarPiecing™ (The Snap Source, Inc.)

Please call or write for our free catalog. Our toll-free number to place an order or obtain a free catalog is 800-258-0929 or please use our regular business telephone 715-445-2214 for editorial comment and further information.

Book Design by Jan Wojtech
Edited by Seiche Sanders
Graphics by The Snap Source, Inc.
Illustrations by Melinda Bylow
Photography by Jeanine Twigg, C.J. Twigg,
        Ross Hubbard, Kris Kandler

Library of Congress Catalog Number:
ISBN 0-87341-668-6

Printed in the United States of America
CIP 98-84106

Acknowledgments

I wish to thank all the individuals and companies who, through their insight, talent and support, contributed to the success of The Snap Source, which, in turn, led to the creation of this book.

The Snap Source staff—Thank you for your hard work and dedication. The Snap Source would not be what it is today with out you—a success!

Jan Hutto—I would be lost without your support, travel companionship, sewing talent and financial wizardry. Thanks for always being there for me.

Kwik Sew Pattern Co.—Thank you for contributing garments for the creation of this book.

Linda McGehee and Sallie J. Russell (the queens of sewing inspiration!)— Thank you for contributing garments and ideas for the creation of this book.

SewBaby!—Thank you contributing the adorable items from your Snap Happy Pattern Collection for inclusion in the book.

Viking Sewing Machine Company—Thank you for providing the #1 Plus.

Thank you to those individuals and companies who have purchased the Snap Source Products. Without your business, quality snap fasteners would not be acknowledged as the ultimate creative closure on the market today.

In addition, I would like to thank the following companies for their generous contributions of the products shown in this book:

- Cactus Punch
- Fasnap Corporation
- HooVer Products
- Prym/Dritz Corporation
- Ready Bias
- The Quilters Binding
- Scovill Fasteners Inc.
- Time-Saver Tool Corporation
- Universal Fasteners Inc.
- Vicar International

Dedication

With thanks to my family and friends for their love and support during the 'snap' years. A debt of gratitude goes to my husband: Thank you for being the most wonderful, supportive and patient husband a hard-working, dedicated, traveling business-owner could ever have as a partner in life!

Table of Contents

Chapter		Projects . . . . Page

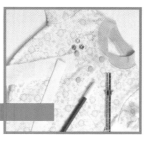

Foreword by Linda F. McGehee

Dear Sewers and Crafters,

Interesting closures have always fascinated me. They could be highly ornate or very basic and simple. But closures add the finishing touch to projects. They make them look professional and, in addition, make them unique and personal. Snaps are a perfect alternative to making button-holes—they are easy to attach and easy to open and close. Snaps are also extremely versatile and can be used for almost anything—home decoration, projects for the physically challenged and children's as well as adult garments.

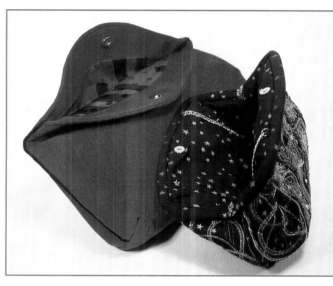

Jeanine has created a book that unlocks the mystery of snaps. From basic knowledge of their development and evolution to the numerous ways to use snaps for the home, games, active wear and eveyday clothing for all ages. She is precise, easy to follow, and full of exciting and inspirational ideas.

The versatility and usefulness of snaps make them a must for every sewer and crafter. Whether for utility or decoration, I know you will enjoy adding snaps to your collection of projects.

—Linda

Author and Speaker Linda F. McGehee is internationally known for her creativity with textiles—from purses to art-to-wear. Her ability to manipulate fabric into works of art can inspire us all to go beyond basic sewing into a whole new world of sewing art. Linda's outstanding and innovative approach to sewing with textiles can be found in her book Creating Texture with Textiles, available from Krause Publications.

The purses shown on this page were designed by Linda. More information can be found in the References section at the end of the book.

In 1990, when sewing for my newborn daughter, I realized there was a difference between the snaps that were found in sewing stores and those found on ready-to-wear garments. After attempting to attach snaps to my carefully made garments, I encountered one or more of the following problems:

- the snaps ripped a hole in the fabric
- the snaps would pop off at inopportune times
- the snap would not stay closed—the snaps kept opening during use
- after laundering the garment, the snaps would mysteriously appear in the bottom of the washing machine or dryer

If you have experienced one or more of these problems, then this book has been written for you. *It's A Snap!* will solve the mysteries of attaching snaps and point you in the right direction for a fun snap attaching experience.

Over the years, I have acquired an in-depth knowledge of snaps and have discovered the secrets behind successful snapping. *It's A Snap!* will uncover the mystery behind a successful snap closure, explain where snaps came from, show you how to identify a quality snap product and determine what snap attaching tool and snaps are best for your sewing or craft project. You'll be amazed at how easy snapping can be—especially with the multitude of fun projects out there waiting for you.

Before we get started there are few things you must know: For the duration of this book, the term "snap fasteners" will be referred to as "snaps." Use the following guides as you would a pattern to help you through the upcoming sewing and craft projects.

Illustration Guide:		Snap Guide:
	Right side of Fabric	Open Prong Ring (opr) or post
	Wrong side of fabric	socket
	Interfaced fabric	stud
	Fashion fabric	cap

Keep in mind that this book is a guide to understanding the basics of snap attaching. There are more than 2,000 different snaps in the world and snaps are uniquely created by each manufacturer. The world of snaps is constantly changing to meet the demands of the industries for which they are intended. So, let's start with a fresh approach and see why snaps are the most misunderstood sewing notion on the market today.

Happy Snapping,

Jeanine

Snap (snap) n. 1: any clasp or fastener that closes with a click v. 2: to close, fasten, go into place, etc. with a snapping sound v. 3: to break, part or be released with a sharp, cracking sound.

It's All in the Name

History of Snaps

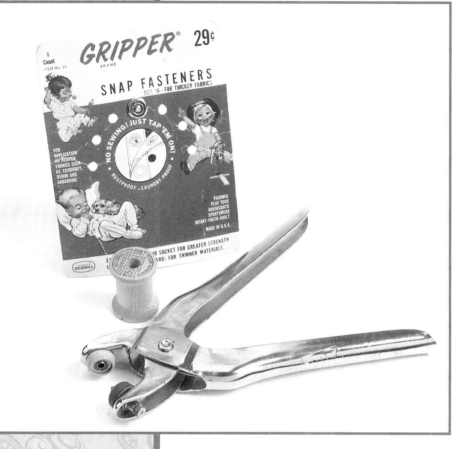

Snaps date back as far as the 1800's when they were used mainly for costumes. Elegant costumes and lingerie were closed with sew-on snaps to make changing quicker and easier. Snaps were developed after the button, but long before the zipper and hook & loop tape.

In the 1800's, sew-on snaps were referred to as "press studs" and "poppers." The term "press stud" was coined by Louis Hannart when he invented the 4-part snap fastener in 1863. It was designed as an improvement to the clasps and fasteners that were then used for gloves and other wearing apparel. In 1885, a spring and stud fastener was invented in Europe and a year later a similar design was patented in the United States, from which the present-day snap evolved.

In the early 1900's, when snap manufacturing in the United States began, manufacturers began calling the innovative closure "snaps," referring to the audible sound made when the snap components clicked into contact with each other. Some of the first manufacturers developed a variety of post-setting snaps as a variation of the button. The most common was a parallel-spring snap that was fashioned after the sew-on snap. See page 12 for more information on snap terminology.

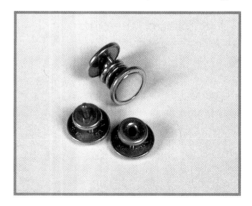

The first snap-links were developed with a parallel-spring closure.

-It wasn't until the 1940's that snaps were introduced into the Home Sewing Industry. Scovill Fasteners Inc. introduced the first Gripper® snap, a prong-style snap that revolutionized the snap manufacturing industry by creating the first snap perfect for infant and children's wear.

Many snap manufacturers created variations of the Gripper snap. The term "Gripper" is Scovill Fastener Inc.'s trade name for their prong-style snap, yet it has become a common term for this type of snap. This causes some confusion in the industry. There are many manufacturers who make this type of snap and market them under different names, such as Snapet®. Most manufacturers simply stamp their company name or trademark symbol on the snap in an effort to differentiate their snap from the competition's.

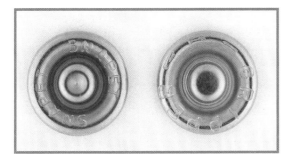

The United States has two major manufacturers of snap fasteners and there are several more scattered throughout the world. However, France, Germany, Italy and the United States have cornered the industrial snap market and have earned a reputation for providing superior snap products. Each snap manufacturer creates snaps in a variety of sizes, styles, finishes and designs. Some even create one-of-a-kind snaps for large garment manufacturers who use them exclusively on one garment line. The best example is outerwear jackets. Jacket snaps vary depending on the coat style and its manufacturer. Therefore, replacing a faulty snap can be a challenging experience! See Chapter 8 for more on snap repair and replacement.

Snap Components

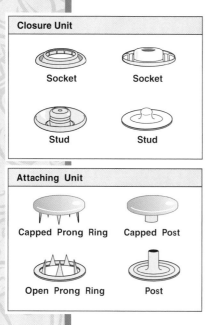

Closure Unit

Socket   Socket

Stud   Stud

Attaching Unit

Capped Prong Ring   Capped Post

Open Prong Ring   Post

Snaps are paired mechanical closures consisting of a closure unit and an attaching unit. A closure unit consists of two different parts—a stud and socket—that must be compatible with each other. Traditionally, studs are attached to the underlap of a garment, while sockets are attached to the overlap of the garment with an attaching unit.

Closure Units:

A Stud is the projecting half of the closure unit with a rim or ball that must fit the socket half of the closure. Studs are available in a variety of diameters, depths and shapes that effect the holding power of the snap. Three common styles are post, prong or staple attached studs.

There are several types of specialty Studs:

Screw Stud: Equipped with a screw for use in metals, plastic or wood.

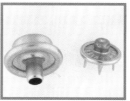

Reversible/Gypsy Stud: Manufactured with an eyelet attached, making it possible for back-to-back assembly with a socket or another stud, or allows you to make a double or reversible closure.

Sockets:
Sockets are the hollow half of the closure unit containing a tension control such as a segmented ring, floating ring or parallel spring to retain the stud. The tension control of the socket and corresponding shape of the stud perform the actual fastening operation.

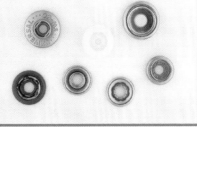

There are several types of sockets:

A Floating Ring Socket expands and contracts inside the rim as the stud is forced into the socket. Ring springs are generally more durable and have greater holding strength.

A Parallel Spring Socket can be identified by the presence of two parallel bars on either side of the socket opening that provide even tension to each side.

A Segmented Ring Socket is are most commonly found in children's wear. The inner ring of the socket is segmented which allows the socket to expand and retract with the insertion of the stud. The more segments, the lighter the tension. Bearded sockets have larger spaces between the segments and are frequently used as the top snap of a garment to allow hair (beard) to pass through the segments without getting caught between the slits.

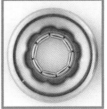

It can be difficult to determine the side of a segmented socket that fits onto the prongs. To do so more easily, place the socket between your thumb and first finger. Move your thumb and finger over the socket to determine which side is slightly raised. The raised side of the socket must go between the fabric and the prong point for a secure attachment.

Attaching Units:

Snaps are clinched in place by attachment parts positioned behind the closure parts. Attachment parts establish the position and provide the holding strength for setting the closure parts. The attachment parts are available in posts, staples or pronged rings—with or without a decorative cap.

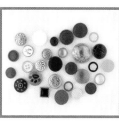

The Cap is the decorative part of the snap and the most visible when the snap is in a closed position. Caps can be produced in any shape or size and consist of a two-part assembly with a post, staple or prong back. Its function is to anchor the socket onto the material and to be decorative or carry a trademark. Caps are made of metal, plastic or a combination and can be antiqued, plated, painted or dyed. Industrial caps are made of high-quality products that guard against scratches or chips that can result from wear.

The Post is the bottom of the snap when it is in the closed position that anchors the stud onto the material. This portion usually rests next to the skin for garment applications and consists of a small or large flange. The post can be self-piercing, which eliminates the need to pre-punch a hole into the garment prior to attaching the snap. These are available with short or long posts. If desirable, a plastic disk can be set with the snap between the fabric and the flange of the post to protect the fabric.

Prong Rings have five inverted triangular shapes formed around a ring designed to self-pierce the fabric. The prongs penetrate the fabric and tunnel into the socket or stud. Prong rings are available in two lengths, short or long, and vary in fineness. Fine prongs are sharper, able to penetrate fabrics with less damage to fibers and are usually longer. Long prongs can be used on thin and thick fabrics to provide more holding power.

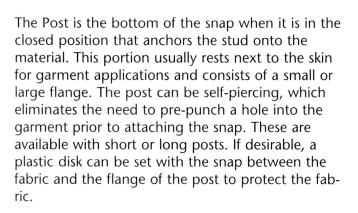

Staples (two-prong fastener) have two prongs that anchor a closing unit onto material. The two-prong fastener cleanly pierces garment material, curls to lock the socket or stud into place and eliminates the pre-punch process.

Snap Materials:

Materials used in producing snaps vary. The most common is brass with a plated finish. Brass is an alloy comprised mostly of copper, zinc and other base metals that have been melted together to create a strong base metal. Traditionally, nickel is the plating of choice, yet there are other finishes such as antique brass, antique silver, antique copper, black nickel and synthetic gold that are also used. Brass does not corrode easily which makes this metal the perfect choice for snap fasteners.

If your water is extremely hard and metals corrode easily, consider a snap made of stainless steel. In addition, stainless steel snaps aid in reducing the chance of allergic reactions to metal called nickel dermatitis. Symptoms of nickel dermatitis include red, round circles on the body where a snap is located on a garment. See Chapter 8 for a quick fix for ready-to-wear garments where one of these snaps already exists.

Plastic Snaps can be molded in all shapes and sizes. Plastic snaps are either molded in colors (which allows the snap to be the same color throughout) or made in the natural color of the plastic—usually white or opaque—then chemically dyed in a hot water bath by the snap manufacturer. When snaps are dyed, the dye adheres to the outside of the plastic but will not chip off. Be careful, though. When snaps that are not dyed properly, the color can fade with washing or become unevenly colored. See Chapter 3: Color Choices for dying snaps at home.

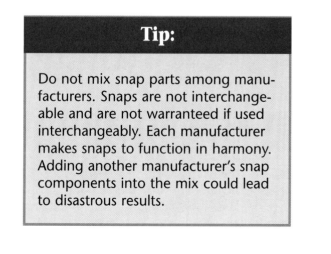

Tip:

Do not mix snap parts among manufacturers. Snaps are not interchangeable and are not warranteed if used interchangeably. Each manufacturer makes snaps to function in harmony. Adding another manufacturer's snap components into the mix could lead to disastrous results.

Different Types of Snaps

Here are just a few of the most popular types of snaps:

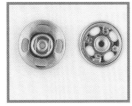

Sew-On: Available as closing units and have holes for sewing on by hand or machine. Sizes vary and are identified by numbers. Sizes 4/0 (0000) to 1/0 (0) are used on sheer and medium-weight fabrics. Sizes 1 to 4 are used on heavier fabrics. Sew-on snaps are available in nickel, brass, black-enameled coated metal, plastic or clear nylon. Clear or transparent plastic snaps are used where a metal snap would detract from the appearance of a garment.

Prong-Style: Available in sets of closing and attaching units with teeth-like grips that penetrate through fabric. The top is either capped or open. An open ring allows the fabric to show through while a capped ring has the look of a button.

Post-Style: Available in set of closing and attaching units with a tube or shaft that requires a hole to penetrate the fabric. With the aid of a steel die, the posts roll outward to secure to the attaching units.

Magnetic: Available as magnetic closing units with a bendable prong backings that pierce the fabric. Used mostly on purses.

Screw-On: Available as a stud unit with a screw backing that can be used to penetrate wood, metal or other surfaces. Used mostly on football helmets, boats and campers.

Snap Tape: Available as a pair of woven tapes with opposing snaps attached at regular intervals. Snaps on tape can be either plastic or metal. Some tapes are dyable for garment color matching.

Pearl: Available with a decorative cap with a metallic rim and a synthetic pearl. They can be dyed a color to correspond with the desired fabric.

Reversible: Used for projects with two right sides, such as reversible vests and pillows. A snap can be reversible if it has two identical components and the closing units will accept either component. In other words, attach a fashion-colored snap top to the stud as well as an identical snap to the socket. This method of attaching snaps is more costly, but gives the project more versatility.

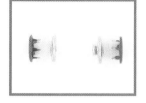

Traditional Closure

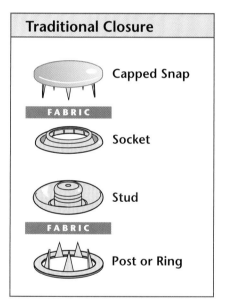

Capped Snap

FABRIC

Socket

Stud

FABRIC

Post or Ring

Reversible Closure

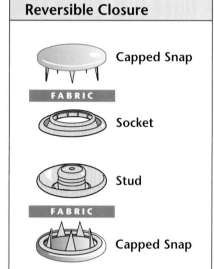

Capped Snap

FABRIC

Socket

Stud

FABRIC

Capped Snap

Snap Sizes

Careful consideration is necessary when choosing the proper snap size for each and every project. With the multitude of snaps on the market finding the perfect snap can be difficult. Here's how to take the confusion out of choosing the best possible snap size.

There are two types of measurement for snaps—inches and millimeters. Snaps manufactured in the United States are measured the same as buttons where increments of 40 lignes (pronounced "lines") are equal to an inch. With this in mind, typical ligne sizes are 16, 18, 20, 24, 27 or approximately 7/16", 17/32", 1/2", 5/8" and 3/4" respectively.

Foreign-made snaps have metric sizing where each snap is measured in millimeters. To determine the metric size of a snap, convert snap size to inches and multiply this number by 25. For example, the Size 20 snap is 1/2", therefore multiply .50 times 25 and the metric equivalent is 12.5 millimeters (13mm).

To convert the millimeter snap size to inches, divide the millimeter snap size by 25. For example, divide 13mm by 25 - the answer is .52, which is close to the Size 20.

If this sounds confusing, don't fret. Most companies have either U.S. or foreign measurements and the chart below will help aid you in snap sizing.

U.S. Sizing (and approximate metric equivalents)

12	14	15	16	18	19	20	24	27
(7.5mm)	(9mm)	(9.5mm)	(10mm)	(11mm)	(12mm)	(13mm)	(16mm)	(19mm)

It's always best to remember that the snaps you choose will most likely only fit the snap attaching tool you purchased with the snaps. For more information on snap attaching products, see Chapter 2.

Here's an example of a long-prong style snap on a heavy weight wool. The longer prongs provide a secure attachment even though the fabric is thicker. Consult Chapter 2 on fabric preparation.

Other than the fact that they appear more substantial, snaps with larger underparts rarely provide more security than snaps with medium-sized underparts. In other words, medium-sized snaps can provide as secure a snap action as larger snaps. Design, fabrics and garment preparation determine the size snap to be used. As a rule for garments, set snaps approximately 3/4" from the edge of the garment front. Use a larger diameter snap cap if the seam allowance will accept a larger snap and use a smaller diameter snap cap for a smaller sea allowance. The fabric guides in Chapter 2 will assist with fabric and snap choices.

When it comes to attaching snaps, there are a multitude of snap attaching products available. To help you choose the best products for your upcoming project, here's some hints and tips for making a snappy decision!

What's Needed for
Snapping Success

Snap Attaching Tools

With the myriad of snap setting devices on the market, it's hard to determine what snap attaching tool is right for you and your project. Don't be surprised to find that you may need to own more than one tool. Not all snap attaching tools work with all snap types. Most hand tools are built for one series, type or style of snap. Industrial presses even need different dies for each style of snap set onto fabric.

See the References section at the end of this book for more information on the companies featured in this photo.

There are several types of snap attaching tools/equipment available today:

- Disposable hammer-based tools
- Hammer-based multi-use tools
- Plier-based, multi-use tools with interchangeable dies
- Table-mounted, hand-operated press with interchangeable dies
- Foot-operated press with interchangeable dies
- Automatic machine press with interchangeable dies

Today, the price of these snap attaching tools can range from "free" with snap purchase, to more than $20,000! For factory installation of snaps, machine presses are used. However, for snap setting at home, a small hand tool is most commonly used. Disposable hammer-based tools come with a package of snaps and can be costly for repeat snapping, but perfect for the one-time snap application.

Choosing a snap attaching tool is like choosing fabric for a garment—the decision is based on personal preference. When it comes to attaching 4-part snaps, a snap attaching device is required.

There are two hand-held tool options for home use—a hammer or plier-based tool. A hammer-based tool is easy on the hands, arms and wrists, especially if arthritis or carpal tunnel syndrome is a factor. It is recommended that you use a firm, flat surface when using hammer-based tools. Instead of hammering on the cement floor of a basement or garage, simply cover a masonry brick completely with cloth and set the small brick over a leg on a sturdy table or workbench. The leg of the table can offer extra support and the hard surface of the brick will provide the necessary stability for setting snaps.

Plier-based tools are more costly, but can provide more setting options due to the inclusion of interchangeable dies. These interchangeable dies will allow one tool to set an array of snap sizes and styles by protecting the snap as it is being set. Be patient with the tool. Allow yourself time to become familiar with the correct dies to use for the different types of snaps the tool can set. Also, practice squeezing the pliers to determine how much pressure is needed to set the snaps properly. Once you have learned how to use the tool properly, you'll have snapping success!

No matter what type of tool is best for you, keep in mind that you will need to use the appropriate snaps for the snap attaching tool(s) you choose. Be sure the snap attaching tool cradles and protects the snap when setting the snap to fabric. Always follow the manufacturer's instructions when using the snap products. If you have questions, contact the manufacturer or the store where the tool was purchased. Allow yourself time to become accustomed to using a snap attaching tool.
Keep in mind that snaps are designed to be attached by factory machinery. The hand tools on the market are made to simulate factory machinery and will provide as close to a factory attached snap as possible. However, because of the precision required, some snaps must be set with factory machinery. Therefore, be aware of these factors and consider using quality snap attaching products and snaps to do your own setting at home.

Quality Snap Products

As with any product on the market, there is always a difference in the quality and construction of each manufacturer's snaps. Be aware that snap components are not interchangeable among manufacturers. Therefore, avoid mixing snap components with another manufacturer's snaps—they may not always work together.

To identify a quality snap product, look for a stamped name or trademark on one of the four snap components. The presence of a name or trademark indicates an industrial snap product. If there are no markings on the snap components, the snap *could be* a generic brand. A generic brand of snap is not generally used in the garment manufacturing process and may not be considered an industrial snap.

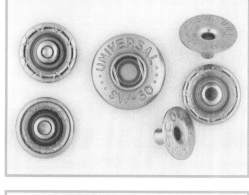

Another method of checking for quality is to look at the shape of the snaps. Be sure all the snap components purchased are shaped identically to one another. On prong-style snaps, check to make sure the underside of the socket and stud have enough of a roll in the metal to secure the prongs when set to fabric. On post-style snaps, check to make sure the hole in the socket and stud are just the right size to accept the post. Too large of a hole will prevent the post from rolling and securing to the socket or stud properly.

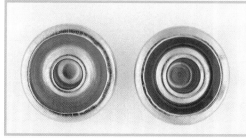

For best results, look for industrial-quality snaps. Attaching snaps with quality products will help make your snapping experience enjoyable and successful. Just remember, if the snap does not set properly, the problem may not be the result of the tool but of the snaps themselves.

The Best Fabrics for Snaps

Choosing the correct fabrics for use with snaps is just as important as choosing the appropriate interfacing for the fabric. As with any garment or craft project, use the fabric guide on the pattern envelope to determine suitable fabrics for the project you are creating. The following is a general guide to matching fabric type with snap style.

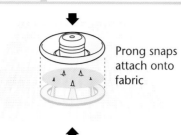

Prong snaps attach onto fabric

Prong-style snap applications:

When using a prong-style snap application, consider using a loosely woven or knit fabric. Use short prong snaps for light-weight fabrics and long-prong snaps for both light-weight and medium-weight fabrics. Fabrics that condense—like Polarfleece®—can accommodate a long-prong snap, too.

Loosely Woven Fabrics	Knit Fabrics
lightweight denim	interlock
quilt cottons	single knit
broadcloth	double knit
shirting	polar-type fabric
flannel	jersey
chambray	lycra
corduroy	

Garment and pattern from Kwik Sew® Pattern Company

Some of the most common uses for prong-style snaps are:
- Dance and skating wear
- Cardigans
- Shirts
- Lightweight jackets
- Polarfleece outerwear
- Children's wear
- Pieced vests
- Western wear
- Home decor
- Costumes
- Uniforms
- Sleepwear

Post-style snap applications:

When using a post-style snap for a heavy application, consider using a densely woven or natural/synthetic fabric. Use a short post for medium-weight fabrics and a long post for medium and heavy-weight fabrics.

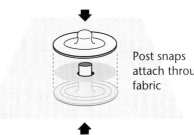

Post snaps attach through fabric

Densely Woven Fabrics	*Natural/Synthetic Fabrics*
heavy weight denim	*fur*
twills	*leather*
awning	*Ultrasuede®*
outerwear flannel	*Ultraleather®*
poplin	

Some of the most common uses for post-style snaps are:
- Leather jackets
- Purses/bags
- RV and Boat covers
- Ski jackets
- Tents
- Fur coats
- Back packs

Tip:

Always apply a practice snap onto a sample of the fabric before sewing the garment. Try opening and closing the sample to check for stability or stress given to the fabric. Adjust the interfacing and snaps accordingly.

Garment and pattern from Kwik Sew® Pattern Company

Fabric Preparation

Choosing the right fabric for a garment or project is as important as choosing the correct interfacing for proper snap attachment. It is recommended that you use an interfacing to help reinforce and protect the fabric surrounding the fasteners.

Fortunately, interfacing decisions are easy. For best results, use a tricot (knit) fusible interfacing or a woven non-fusible interfacing. Use a tricot fusible interfacing when choosing knit or light-woven fabric. However, if

you are attaching snaps across the stretch of knit fabric, use a woven interfacing in this area. For all other fabrics, use a woven non-fusible interfacing.

The easiest woven non-fusible interfacing to obtain is bleached or unbleached muslin that is found at most quilt shops. Look for a muslin that has a loose weave to the fabric. If a project is not translucent in color (white/pastels), use left-over quilt fabric from a project. Interfacing is used on the inside of a garment and will not be visible from the outside of the project.

For best results, pre-shrink 100% cotton quilt fabrics or woven, non-fusible interfacing. Serge or finish the raw edges, then wash the piece in mild soap or detergent. Dry the piece in the dryer on a medium heat to remove the moisture (10 minutes or so). Remove the piece from the dryer and press with a dry iron to remove creases and excess moisture.

In addition, pre-shrink the knit fusible tricot interfacing. Using a small bucket, soak the tricot interfacing in warm water for 3-5 minutes. Remove the interfacing from the water and gently squeeze out the excess water. Lay the interfacing on a clean, dry towel. Roll up the towel with the interfacing inside. Squeeze the towel to absorb the excess water, then unroll the towel and remove the interfacing. Drape the interfacing over a hanger to dry.

Twill tape and bias tape may also be used to interface the diaper opening area of children's clothing and other areas of garments that endure stress. Consider using 100% cotton twill tape. Cotton holds up best through repeat washings, but requires pre-shrinking. To pre-shrink, simply soak the twill for 10 minutes in a bowl of warm water. Remove the twill tape from the bowl and lie flat on a clean, dry towel. Roll up the towel with the twill tape inside. Twist the towel slightly, unroll the towel and remove the twill tape. Drape the twill tape over a hanger to dry. When the twill tape is dry, press with a dry iron to remove the wrinkles.

Pre-punch holes in fabric

There are a variety of hole-punching devices available for making holes in projects to accept the post-style snaps. When punching holes in fabric, first determine where the snap will be placed and punch through all layers at the same time to avoid misalignment. The most readily available punch is an awl or an awl-like punch that is used in conjunction with a small rotary cutting board or piece of wood. Some punches come with sewing machines for eyelet making and some come with plier-based tools. Whichever hole punch you choose, be sure to make the hole smaller than the post of the snap.

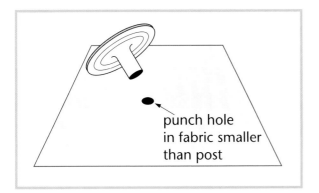

punch hole in fabric smaller than post

Pattern and garment from Kwik Sew® Pattern Company

Pre-sewn eyelet for knit fabrics

Even if your fabric is interfaced properly, there is the possibility that a snap will pull through knit fabric when you use post-style snaps. To prevent this from happening, use a sewing machine to sew an eyelet where the snap is to be set. After the machine eyelet is sewn onto the fabric, punch a hole in the center of eyelet, taking care not to cut the stitches. Then set the snap according to the manufacturer's instructions.

machine eyelet

Snap Alignment

As with buttons and buttonholes, precision is needed when aligning the snaps to both sides of the garment or project. When setting post-style snaps, the alignment is crucial. Snap alignment must be determined before the holes are punched. If a snap is moved to a new location, the old hole remains. When setting prong-style snaps, the alignment is not as crucial. Prong-style snaps can be removed and a new snap can be attached without harm to fabric. No matter what method you choose, if a mistake is made attaching snaps, do not reuse snap components. The snap is damaged and may not function correctly if reset.

There are several notions available for marking.
- Water-soluable marking pen
- Chalk pencil or tailor's chalk
- Soap sliver (no lotion soaps!)

Mark the fabric with an "X" or dot where the snap is to be set to the project. For polar-type or fabrics with a nap, use chalk or a water-soluable marking pen with an easy applicator. This will make it easy to mark over the nap of fabrics. When using a chalk pencil found in an artist supply store, dip the pencil in a cup filled with only a 1/4" of water. This will make the pencil easier to use and more legible when marking the fabric.

Several methods can be used to align snaps. Here are some suggestions:

1 Tape Marking: Affix masking tape to the front overlap 3/4" away from the front edge and directly on the front and bottom edge. Identify where the snap will be set to the project. Mark the masking tape with a horizontal double arrow line across the width of the tape where snaps will be attached to the fabric. Then, using a fabric marking utensil, mark the fabric with a dot next to the arrow on the tape. Remove the masking tape and align the tape on the underlap of the closure in the same manner as the overlap. Mark the fabric and remove the tape. Attach snaps according to the manufacturer's instructions.

2 Socket Marking: Identify and mark the location where the fashion colored snap and socket will be set onto fabric. Attach these snap components to the overlap of the front closure. Arrange the garment in the closed position, aligning the overlap over the underlap where the stud and open ring will be set. Gently lift up the overlap and rub each attached socket with chalk and press the socket onto the underlap. The chalked socket will create a mark on the underlap. This mark is where the stud and open ring should be set. (Note: These instructions can be used to mark the stud as well.)

3 Pin Marking: Spread the garment onto a large padded surface. Arrange the garment in the closed position, aligning the overlap over the underlap where the snaps will be set. Identify and mark the location where the fashion colored snap and socket will be set onto the fabric. Using dressmaking pins, insert them into fabric through all the layers at each mark on the garment. Gently pick up the overlap and mark the location where the pin penetrates the fabric. These markings will identify were the snaps are to be set.

Trouble Shooting

If you're having difficulty attaching a snap, here are some helpful hints to ensure snapping success.

Do not attach snaps over stitching or a seam. The bulk of the stitching or seam that adds to the closure area may get in the way of a secure attachment. Simply move the snap to avoid the stitching or seam.

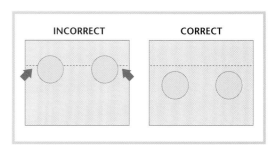

Do not attach snaps on an uneven thickness of fabric. The uneven fabric prevents a secure attachment. Simply move the snap to an even thickness of fabric.

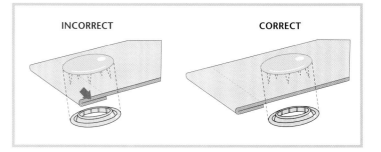

Prong-style snaps

Be sure a fingernail cannot be forced between fabric and the closure unit. If the snap is not set tightly to the fabric, place the snap back into the snap attaching tool and continue the application until the snap is properly set.

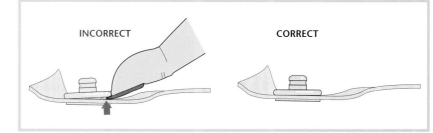

Be sure the prongs are not protruding from beneath the closure unit. If a prong is exposed, remove and discard the incorrectly set snap. Start the snapping process again.

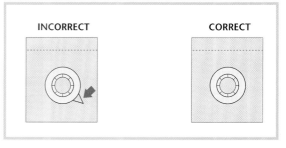

Post-setting snaps

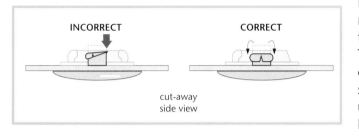

INCORRECT   CORRECT

cut-away
side view

Be sure the post rolls properly onto the closure unit. The post should be evenly rolled to secure the closure unit to the fabric. In addition, be sure the socket and stud have the proper opening for the post. An opening that is too large will also cause difficulty in setting the snap. There is a possibility that the snap will not close properly if the post is not rolled correctly.

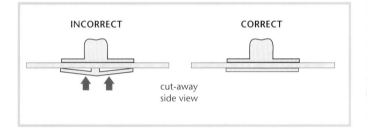

INCORRECT   CORRECT

cut-away
side view

Be sure the bottom of the post is flat next to the fabric. If the snap is not set tightly to the fabric, place the snap on the fabric into the snap attaching tool and continue the application until the snap is properly set.

Staple-setting snaps

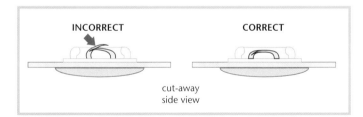

INCORRECT   CORRECT

cut-away
side view

Be sure the prongs are curled properly onto the closure unit. The prongs should be evenly curled to secure the closure unit to the fabric. There is a possibility that the snap will not close properly if the prongs are not curled correctly.

When it comes to design changes, the possibilities are endless. Let's begin by adding a little snap to your creative projects—from simple pattern changes to snapping up bulky fabrics.

Design Changes for Snaps

Snappy Pattern Changes

Have you ever wished a pattern had just the right closure you were looking for? Or, have you ever found the perfect pattern—except it called for a zipper? Well, look no further, here's how you can alter a pattern to include just the right closure you're looking for...snaps!!!

What you will need:

Pattern tracing material
Pattern to be altered
Measuring utensil
Fashion fabric
Interfacing
Matching thread
Long prong-style snaps
Snap attaching tool

1 Locate the center front on the pattern piece of the garment to be created.

2 Using your favorite pattern-tracing material, outline the pattern piece from the center front outward. Add 1-1/2" to 2" to the center front for the front extensions and facing. Cut 1-1/2" to 2" from the fashion fabric.

3 Identify the best interfacing to use with the fabric you have chosen (See Chapter 2). On the wrong side of fabric, interface 1" to 1-1/4" of the extension starting from the cut edge. Overcast raw edges.

4 Fold the facing to the wrong side of the garment at the edge of the interfacing. Attach snaps according to manufacturer's instructions. Be sure to overlap the front correctly—left to right for women and right to left for men.

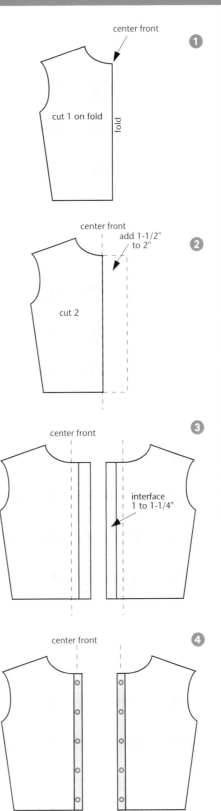

Snapping Basic:

The fashion-colored snap and socket is attached to the overlap. The stud and open ring are attached to the underlap. The fashion-colored snap top is shown on the outside of the garment. The back component is on the inside next to the body. And, the socket and stud are the closure units.

There may be times when a closure is preferred in only a part of the garment. For example, instead of a shoulder closure on an infant onesie, try re-designing the pattern to offer a closure down the front of the garment.

❶ Using your favorite tracing material, outline the pattern piece to be altered. Cut the traced pattern at the desired location to be separated.

❷ Retrace the two pattern pieces and add back in the 1/4" seam allowance at the cut edge. Add 1-1/2" to 2" to the center front for the front extension and facing. Using the pattern piece for adding snaps (top front), cut 2 from the fashion fabric. Using the pattern piece with the fold (bottom front), cut 1 from the fashion fabric.

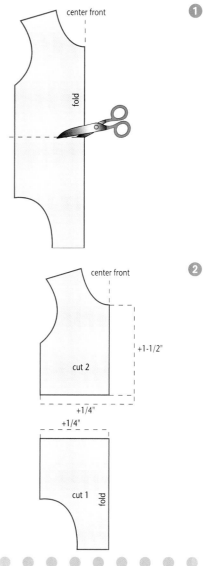

3 Identify the best interfacing to use with the fabric chosen. See Chapter 2 for more information on interfacing options. On the wrong side of the fabric (top front) interface 1" to 1-1/4" of the extension starting from the cut edge. Overcast raw edges.

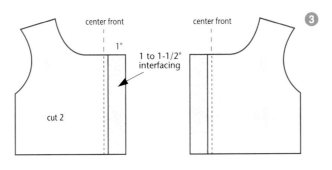

4 Fold the facing to the wrong side of the garment at the edge of the interfacing. Overlap the top front left and top front right together. Be sure to overlap the front correctly—left to right for girls and right to left for boys.

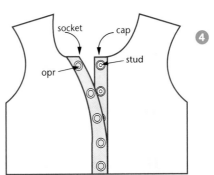

With right sides together, stitch top front to top bottom using a 1/4" seam allowance. Attach snaps according to manufacturer's instructions.

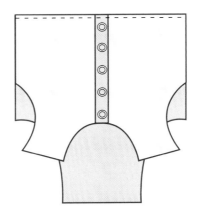

5 Use the redesigned front to construct the remainder of the garment according to pattern instructions. Remember to use a front-opening neck binding method.

Note: Snaps can be attached before or after the top and bottom are sewn together.

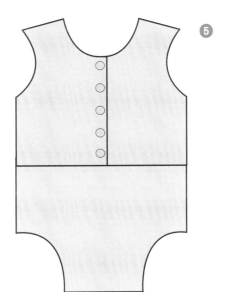

Sew Easy Snap Tape

There are several advantages to making your own snap tape—you can save money, color-coordinate the tape to your project and choose where snaps are set. Here's how to start getting creative with snaps—plus save money—by making your own snap tape.

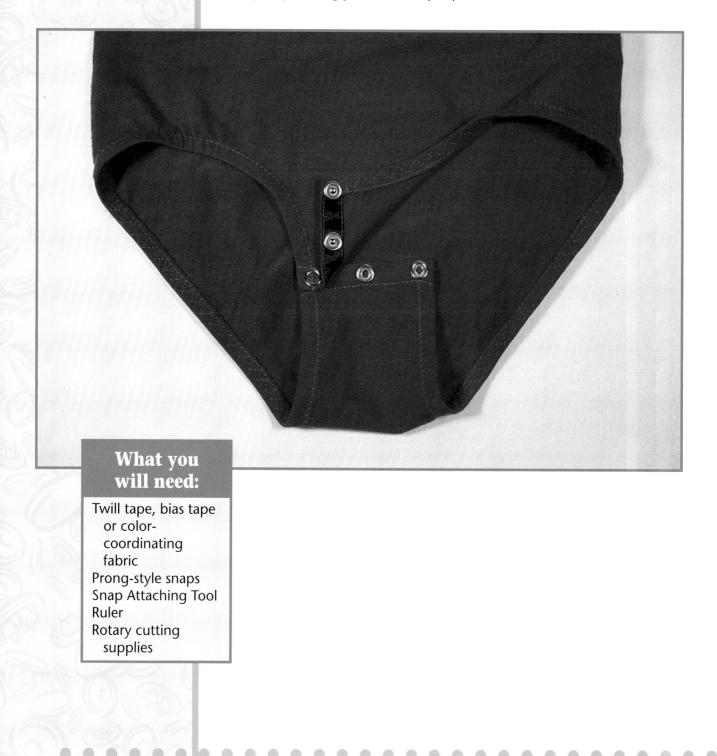

What you will need:

Twill tape, bias tape or color-coordinating fabric
Prong-style snaps
Snap Attaching Tool
Ruler
Rotary cutting supplies

Snap tape can be used on everything from infant wear to home decor. The best fabric to use for the tape fabric is the left-over material (scraps) from the project. Use a rotary cutter for best results.

1 When using knit fabrics, cut 1-1/4" strips parallel to the selvage of the fabric as illustrated.

2 When using woven fabric, cut 1-1/4" strips on the bias (45 degree angle) as shown.

3 Use as much scrap fabric as possible for the tape. If necessary, sew the pieces together to form a continuous strip. To piece the strips of knit or woven fabric, square off the ends of each section. With right sides together, join cut edges on a 45 degree angle. Stitch from corner to corner as shown.

4 Trim within a 1/4" from the stitching line and finger press open.

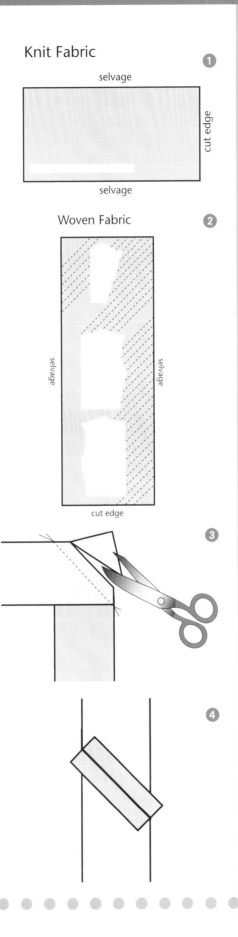

Knit Fabric **1**

selvage

cut edge

selvage

Woven Fabric **2**

selvage

selvage

cut edge

3

4

Attaching Snap Tape

When attaching either purchased or self-made fabric strips, bias-tape or twill tape, keep in mind the pattern instructions for the garment. If the pattern has a fabric fold-under facing, you can choose two different sewing methods. Either follow the pattern instructions and interface the self-fabric facing, or consider trimming all but 1/4" from the fold line to accommodate the attachment of the fabric strip of choice. Here's how to attach the pre-made fabric strips to just about any pattern style. Adding fabric strips to the diaper opening of an infant garment is illustrated.

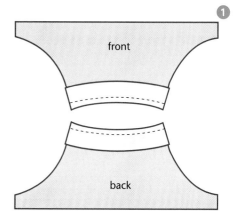

❶ If necessary, trim all but 1/4" from the fold line of the garment. Measure the diaper opening area at the 1/4" stitching line. Cut strips of pre-made fabric, twill or bias tape the corresponding length plus 1/2" for the finished edge. Stitch fabric strips onto the right side of fabric using a 1/4" seam allowance.

❷ Understitch seam allowance to the fabric strip.

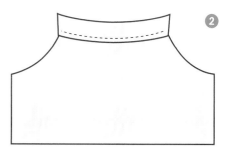

Tip:

Follow pattern instructions for garment construction. There may be times when the fabric strips are topstitched down after snaps are set. Each pattern company may assemble and use snap tape differently.

3 Baste 1/4" from raw edge.

4 Turn under raw edges at stitching line, press and top stitch close to the folded edge.

5 Attach snaps according to manufacturer's instructions. Be sure to use the correct snap components as illustrated.

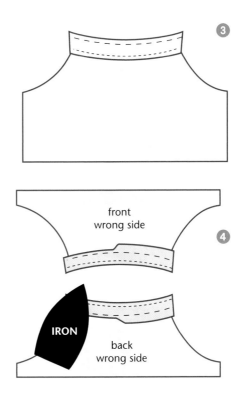

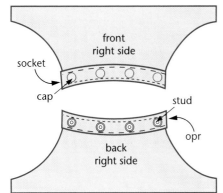

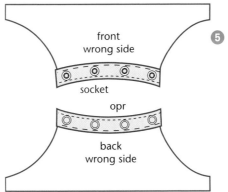

Snapping Up Bulky Fabric

Snaps and bulky fabrics make a great combination if care is used when preparing the fabric. For example, polar-type fabrics are bulky but the loft of the fabric will condense to accept a snap. With the correct fabrics, interfacing and snap products, the task of attaching snaps can produce wonderful results. If the fabric is prepared correctly, a long prong-style snap is the best choice for the closure.

Before starting a project with bulky fabric, consider re-checking the choices made in the fabric, pattern and accessories for the garment.

Here are just some of the questions you might want to ask yourself before starting the project:

• Does the pattern call for the fabric selected?
• Is the pattern design "roomy or oversized" to accommodate the bulk of the fabric?
• Do you have all the sewing notions to start the project?
• Does the pattern call for a zipper, buttons or snaps?

If the fabric chosen is not on the suggested fabric list of the pattern, can the project be made one size larger to accommodate the bulk? Consider looking at the pattern and determine where the bulk of the fabric can be eliminated to reduce the thickness of the seams.

Here's an example of a pattern that calls for bulky fabric.

There are four places where the fabric bulk can be eliminated. By removing the bulk, the garment will lay smoother on the body and add stability to the fabric for snap attaching.

1 Cut the collar from the bulky fabric and cut the under collar from two layers of a coordinating, woven quilt cotton. The second layer of quilt cotton will act as the stabilizer.

2 Cut the facing of the garment from two layers of a coordinating, woven quilt cotton. One layer will be the facing and one layer will be the interfacing.

3 As with the collar, cut one tab from the bulky fabric and the other from two layers of a coordinating, woven quilt cotton.

The pocket is the fourth location for bulk removal. See page 46 for instructions on how to sew patch pockets on bulky fabric.

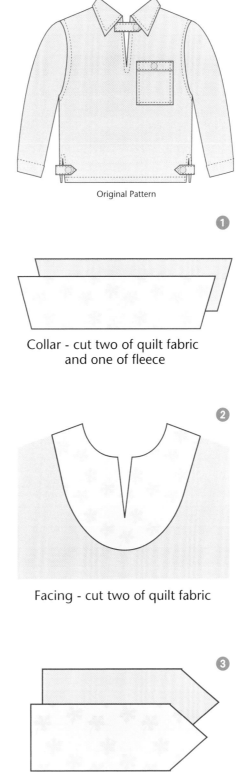

Original Pattern

1

Collar - cut two of quilt fabric
and one of fleece

2

Facing - cut two of quilt fabric

3

Tab - cut two of quilt fabric
and one of fleece

Patch Pockets on Bulky Fabric

1 When it comes to patch pockets on bulky fabrics, simply cut off all but 1/4" from the fold on the pocket. Cut 2 strips of coordinating woven quilt fabric 1-1/2" to 2" by the width of the pocket for use as the pocket facing and interfacing.

2 With the woven fabric wrong sides together and on the right side of the pocket, stitch all layers together using a 1/4" seam allowance.

3 Understitch the seam allowance to the facing.

4 Turn facing to the wrong side, topstitch down and add a snap.

Follow the manufacturer's remaining instructions for securing the pocket to the garment.

Tip:

These instructions work for all aspects of pocket sewing. It's a great way of making sure a pocket head does not stretch out of shape. For polar-type fabrics, use pinking or scalloping scissors on the raw edges and topstitch pocket onto garment for a decorative, fun look.

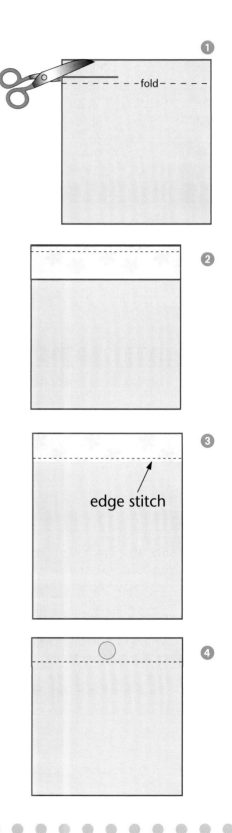

1 — fold — —

2

3 edge stitch

4

Fabric Compression

When using polar-type fabrics, one way to make snap attaching easier is to compress the fabric with the sewing machine before the snap is set. This can be done by making a stitched "x", "o" or "+" to compress the fabric layers together.

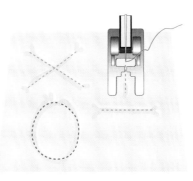

Identify and mark the location where the snap components will be attached. Set the sewing machine to a medium stitch length and stitch a desired symbol to the overlap and underlap on the markings. Be sure to compress and mark the fabric smaller than the snap size.

Facing Alternatives

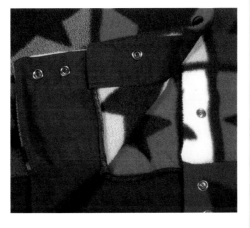

If a large, faced pattern requires more than a simple alteration to eliminate the bulk, try this method to alter the pattern. You'll be amazed at how nice the garment looks by eliminating the bulk of the fabric. By adding the lighter layer of fabric as the garment facing, the bulk is reduced from the closure area allowing the snaps to penetrate the fabric with added stability.

❶ If the pattern calls for a fold-over facing, trim the facing to within a 1/4" from the front fold line.

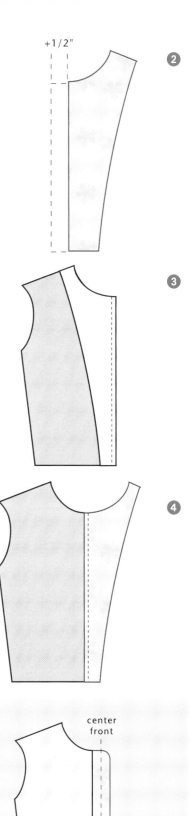

2 Retrace the cut-away facing and add 1/2" to the cut edge. Cut four new front facings from a fashion coordinating woven fabric such as quilt cotton. Two cut pieces will be for the facing and two cut pieces will be for the interfacing.

3 With right sides together, stitch the interfaced facings to the garment with a 1/4" seam allowance.

4 Understitch the seam allowance to the facing and overcast the unfinished edge of the facing as desired. Turn the facing to the inside of the garment. Do not press: The understitching will keep the facing in place.

An Alternative:

Completely trim off the facing at the fold line. Cut four strips of complimentary woven fabric (or two heavy-weight fabric) 1-1/2" wide by the length of the garment front. Overcast one edge of the fabric strip. With wrong sides together, baste the strip to the garment matching the raw edge of the strip with the cut edge of the garment front. When the seams of the garment are completed, stitch bias trim to the outer edges of the neck and front. Be sure to catch the facing in the bias trim. Remove basting stitches and attach snaps according to the manufacturer's instructions.

Post-style Snaps on Polar-type Fabrics

When setting a post-style snap to polar-type fabrics, use a woven fabric to surround both sides of the garment underlap and overlap to create a woven placket. The most commonly used fabric is Supplex. The woven fabric sandwiches the polar-type fabric and absorbs the stress the fabric endures from the snap use. Pre-punch the hole through all layers to accommodate the post-setting snap.

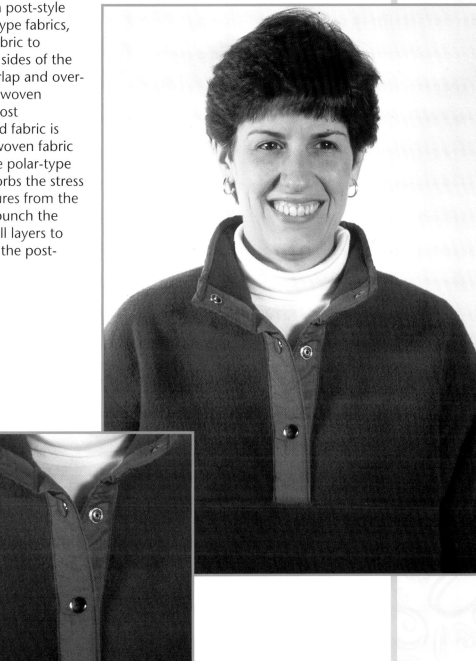

Snap on a Button!

Here's a fun idea for just about any fabric, but the idea works best on polar-type fabrics. Try adding a plain prong ring snap to polar-type fabrics. Then, sew on a button for this clever Snappy-Button closure!

What you will need:

Polar fabric
Open Ring Snaps
 with Long Prongs
Snap Attaching Tool
Hand-Sewing
 Needle
Shank buttons
Matching thread

❶ Identify and mark the fabric where the open ring snaps are to be set to the garment. Attach the snaps according to the manufacturer's directions. Be sure to use the correct snap components as illustrated.

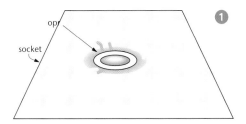

2 By using an open-ring, prong-style snap, the ring of the snap creates a well and a tuft of fabric as illustrated.

3 This tuft of fabric protruding from the ring is perfect for sewing on a shank button. Using a needle and thread, attach the thread to the tuft of fleece.

4 Hand sew on the decorative button. It's best to use a small shank button, where the button covers the snap no more than a 1/2" in diameter.

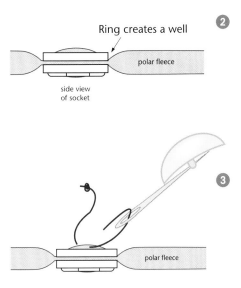

Ring creates a well

polar fleece

side view
of socket

polar fleece

polar fleece

Snap 'n' Flower Appliqué

As a fun idea for kids of all ages, try cutting a flower from polar-type fabrics and attach the flower to the front overlap with the fashion-colored snap top.

What you will need:

Scrap piece of Polar Fabric
Long Prong Snaps
Snap Attaching Tool
Scissors

Color Choices

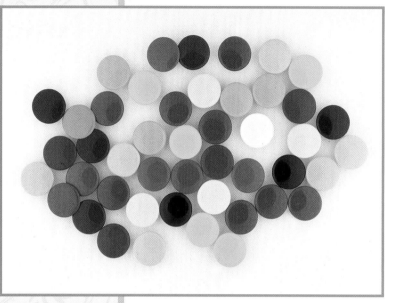

The closure of any project is the finishing touch that can make a project spectacular. Adding color to projects with snaps can be exciting. Here's some fun and creative ideas to add a little color to your upcoming project.

Colorful Snap Closures

Most sources package snaps with 6 to 12 complete sets of snaps. Again, remember not to mix snap components (See Chapter 1 for more details). Keep different manufacturers' snaps separated. To keep snaps organized, consider using a compartment box found at a hardware store or an embroidery floss keeper found at a hobby store. As your collection of snaps increases, you may find one or two leftover snaps in several different colors. If the colors coordinate, use the varied colors on a garment or project. This design touch is used in ready-made clothing and can be a fun accent for any project.

Color-Coordinating Snaps and Fabric

Locating a snap to match a project perfectly can be difficult, especially if the color is unusual. Consider using a complimentary color to coordinate with the fabric instead of attempting to match the exact color. For example, it is difficult to find a denim-colored snap. Pastel Blue is too light, Royal Blue doesn't match and Navy Blue is too dark. Try using a complimentary antique metal finish such as Antique Brass, Antique Copper or Antique Silver—especially if the color coordinates with the topstitching thread. Consider always having these colors on hand for the times when the perfect match cannot be found.

Dyeable Snaps

There are two types of snaps that can be dyed.

- Pearl Snaps
- Plastic Snaps

Both pearl and plastic snaps have non-porous, synthetic features that enable the appropriate dye to adhere to the outside of the material. The dying of snaps can be done at home on the kitchen stove. Choose a dye that is hot-water activated and is made for synthetic products. Dyes made for cotton fibers will not adhere to the plastic properly and will eventually fade resulting in a disastrous look over time.

It's best to use a powder dye, but make sure the dye is completely dissolved in the hot water before placing the snaps in the solution. Do not let the water boil or it will ruin the dye process. Continuously stir the snaps in the dye bath using a plastic disposable spoon until the dye has changed the snap to the desired color. Be sure to rinse snaps in cold water thoroughly and set aside to dry completely.

As with any product, read the manufacturer's directions completely before starting the dying process. To ensure satisfactory results, follow the directions exactly. Consider purchasing an extra package of snaps for experimental purposes.

Pocket Snaps

When it comes to pockets, snaps are the easiest closure! Attach a large, colorful snap to a flip top style pocket. Simply add a snap or a snap tab to a welt pocket that won't stay closed. You can even try using snaps instead of topstitching. Snap up some fun to your next pocket project!

1 Attach snaps according to the manufacturer's instructions. Be sure to use the correct snap components as illustrated.

2 To use a snap instead of topstitching, attach the snaps according to the manufacturer's instructions, through all thicknesses of the garment and pocket. Be sure to use a long-prong snap for the maximum holding power and the correct snap components as illustrated.

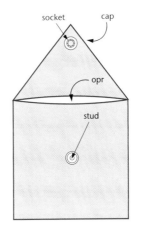

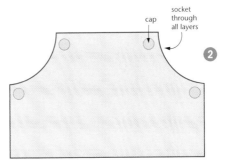

Snappy PolarPiecing™

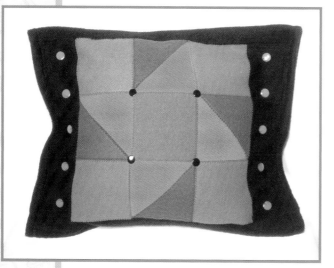

Have you every wondered what to do with all your leftover polar-type fabric pieces after cutting out a garment? Don't throw your left over fabric away—try this fun, creative idea coined by Jeanine Twigg called PolarPiecing™. It's a great way to achieve a designer detail when using scraps of polar-type fabrics.

What is PolarPiecing™? PolarPiecing is a quilting technique that adjoins polar-type scraps together into usable fabric pieces.

What you will need:

Scrap pieces of polar-type fabrics
Sewing machine with multi-motion stitches
Black or dark colored thread to coordinate
Prong-style snaps
Rotary cutting supplies

The polar-type fabrics available today are warm, plush and full of design possibilities. The great quilting potential of this wonderful fabric can dramatically change the look of any sewing project. The idea behind PolarPiecing™ is to piece geometric shapes together—as you would in quilting—to create fabric for use in garments, home dec, toys and more.

How to PolarPiece™

① Using different colors of polar-type fabric, cut shapes that fit together such as squares, triangles, rectangles or consult your favorite quilting reference book for design possibilities.

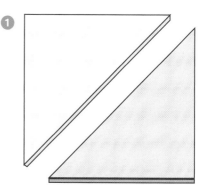

② Adjoin the cut pieces together using decorative machine stitches directly under the pressure foot of your sewing machine. Do not over-lap seams—abut the cut edges with stitches that multi-stitch on both sides of the adjoined pieces. Multi-motion, decorative stitches are best to use in order to secure the pieces together.

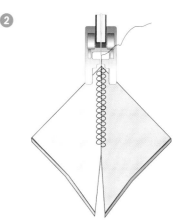

③ Use simple decorative stitches at least 4 mm in width. A standard zigzag stitch does not have enough stability to hold the raw edges together. Here are some examples of just a few of the many stitches available that are perfect for Polar-Piecing™.

④ PolarPiecing™ and snaps make a great combination. Use the fashion colored snap top and socket as shown in the center for two purposes—for decoration, and to stabilize the intersections of the pieced fabric. The prong points draw all the edges together and reinforce the intersections. They are also great for covering up any misalignment mistakes that could happen as you perfect the technique. Snap as you go. As soon as there is a section to snap, it is best to snap before the pieced fabric gets too large. Attach snaps according to manufacturer's directions.

For best results with PolarPiecing™, use polar-type fabrics with minimal stretch. It is not necessary to keep track of the nap of the fabric for this method of piecing. This will help you when choosing and determining what scraps to use. Consult your fabric quilting book for templates and ideas for piecing. Experiment with simple 4″ squares of different colors. Cut the squares on the diagonal to form triangles, then piece back together the triangles after switching around the colors. Make sure each triangle is pieced with a different color. Then, piece the squares together to create your one-of-a-kind first PolarPieced™ project!

③

④

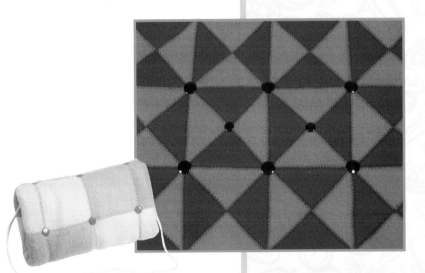

Tip:

For more detailed information on sewing with this versatile fabric, read *Adventures with Polarfleece®: A Sewing Expedition*, by Nancy Cornwell. *Available from Krause Publications.*

To use this PolarPiecing™ method for garment construction, simply create the pieced fabric larger than the garment pattern piece. Cut out the pattern using the pieced fabric as you would fabric off the bolt. It's that simple.

Let's get snap-ping! We'll start our series of fun snap projects with kids' accessories. You'll have so much fun snapping up for kids that soon you'll be dreaming up more snap-filled projects for everything from home decor to evening wear!

Snap Happy Kids

Table-Top Learning Center

Kids love to learn and there is nothing more special than teaching a toddler their ABC's and 1-2-3's. Modeled after a dress created by Sallie J. Russell from SJR Sew with Class, this interactive Learning Center is all about teaching not only the basic fundamentals, but hand-eye coordination as well. Add more letters and the Learning Center can grow with a child to become a Spelling Center. You can even add shapes—the possibilities are endless.

What you will need:

Fashion fabric
Batting
Binding fabric
Marking instrument
Craft foam
Narrow ribbon
Snap Strip
   (See page 75)
Matching thread
36 or more sets of
   prong-style snaps
Snap attaching tool

1 Cut one rectangle 28″ x 11″ from the fashion fabric for the back of the game. Cut one rectangle of batting 28″ x 11″.
For the pieced top of the game, cut three strips 28″ long by 4″ wide.

Mark the fabric strips 1-1/4″ from the cut edge starting approximately 1-3/4″ from the selvedge. This will determine where snaps will be set onto fabric. Attach snaps according to the manufacturer's instructions. Be sure to use the correct snap components as illustrated.

2 With right sides together, sew strips using a 1/4″ seam allowance. Finger press the seams flat.

3 Layer the rectangles as follows, matching cut edges.

4 Slightly round the corners for ease in adding binding.

5 Pin and stitch ribbon over seams through all layers of the pieced top-game fabric.

6 Using your favorite quilt binding method, stitch a binding around the square to seal raw edges. (Consult your favorite quilting instructional book for details.)

7 To make the Learning Center portable, attach snap strips to the back as shown. See page 75 to make the snap strips.

Trace and cut at least 26 letters and 10 numbers from craft foam. Or, consider embroidering letters and numbers onto washable felt as pictured. Cut felt around letters and numbers in shapes for an enhanced teaching element. Attach snaps according to manufacturer's instructions onto craft foam or felt. Find patterns to trace letters and numbers on page 150.

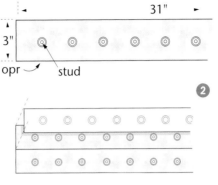

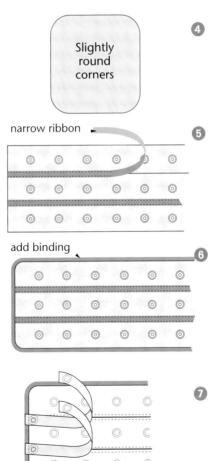

Tip:
Look for snap templates on page 150 and check your local craft store in the "Creative Memories" section. There are several basic templates that will work as well as snap templates.

Snap 'n' Appliqué

There is nothing more fun for kids than a custom-made garment that they can take part in decorating. Use this idea for holiday themes, such as Halloween, St. Patrick's Day or just for some Spring-Time fun. The illustrated sample is for Valentine's Day.

What you will need:

Specially sewn or purchased sweatshirt
Craft foam, Ultra Suede®, or washable felt pieces
Marking utensil
Prong-style snaps
Tricot interfacing
Snap attaching tool

1 Mark the location where snaps are to be set onto specially sewn or purchased sweatshirt. Trace and cut shapes from the craft foam, Ultra-Suede®, or washable felt pieces. Attach snaps according to manufacturer's instructions in the center of each shape. Be sure to use the correct snap components as illustrated.

2 Cut one 1" square of tricot interfacing for each snap that will be set to the sweatshirt. Before attaching the snap to the garment, feed the interfacing squares, with fusible side up, over the prongs of the non-colored open ring. Attach snaps according to manufacturer's instructions onto the sweatshirt. Be sure to use the correct snap components as illustrated.

3 After all the snaps are set onto the sweatshirt, fuse the interfacing squares to the shirt. If necessary, use a press cloth to protect the fabric.

Try this idea for adults, too!
See page 97 for more details.

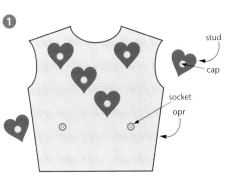

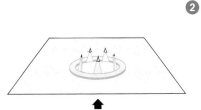

Tip:

For all projects that require snaps to be set in the middle, make sure your snap attaching tool is able to reach into the innermost areas.

Decorative Closures

There are many ways to close a garment—from buttons to snaps to zippers. Why not jazz up an ordinary closure into a closure with snap-pizzazz!

Fabric Knot

Cut two rectangles or ovals approximately 8″ long by 2-1/2″ wide from a lightweight woven fabric. Finish the raw edges by stitching with right sides together, leaving an opening, then turn to the right side. Press.

Attach the snaps through the rectangle onto the front of the garment, according to manufacturer's instructions. Be sure to use the correct snap components as illustrated.

Tie a square knot where the two ends of the rectangle are lying on the fabric perpendicular to the finished edge of the garment.

A designer note: A lightweight, reversible ribbon can be used as well.

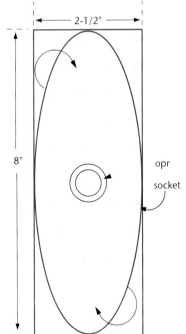

2-1/2″

8″

opr

socket

Tie on a Button

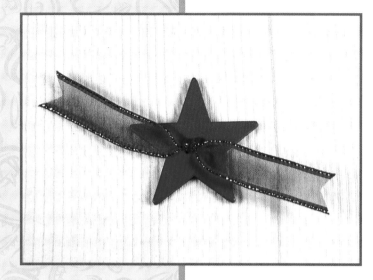

For this project it is extremely important to use an open ring snap set. Therefore, be sure to use the correct snap components as illustrated. Attach the open prong ring snap sets according to manufacturer's instructions onto the garment.

❶ Set your sewing machine to a "0" stitch length and "2" for stitch width. Place the ribbon under the pressure foot as illustrated and carefully zigzag the ribbon onto the garment through the hole in the open prong ring and socket only.

❷ Feed the ribbon through the holes in the button. Tie a knot or bow with the ribbon to secure the button. Allow the ribbon ends to dangle as long as desired.

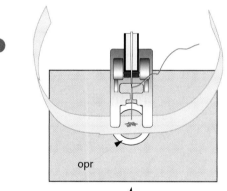

❶

opr

socket

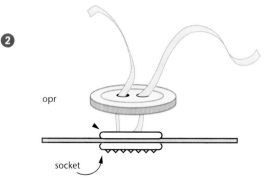

❷

opr

socket

Novelty Bow

Use a snap as the center to a bow. It's a creative way to snap up a closure.

❶ To form a bow with lightweight ribbon, set the bow through the prongs of the snap to secure the gathering of the center of the bow.

❷ Attach snaps according to manufacturer's instructions to set the snap through the bow onto the front of the garment. Be sure to use the correct snap components as illustrated.

❶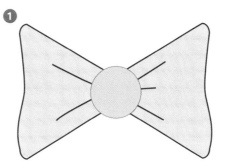

❷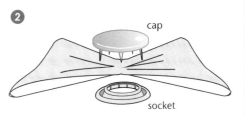

cap

socket

Snap-Off Vest

Again, thanks to Sallie J. Russell's creative talents, here's a fun detachable vest for kids of all ages—including adults. This idea is great for quilters, too. Make one vest and snap it from garment to garment!

1 Choose a pattern that is suitable for the project that includes a lining for the vest. Follow the pattern instructions to sew the front portion of the vest. Stitch wrong sides together leaving an opening for turning. Turn the vest fronts to the right side and topstitch. Attach snaps according to manufacturer's instructions to set the fashion colored snap and stud to the vest at shoulder and side seams. Be sure to use the correct snap components as illustrated. Measure the area where the snaps are set.

2 To stabilize the specially made or purchased shirt, use four finished rectangles made from leftover fabric or four finished pieces of twill tape the same length as the snap area plus 1". Attach snaps according to manufacturer's instructions to set the stud and open ring. Be sure to use the correct snap components as illustrated.

3 Stitch the finished rectangles or twill tape to the specially made or purchased shirt as shown. Be sure to align the strips to the vest where the vest will be snapped to the shirt. Stitch in between the snaps to secure the strips to the shirt. Snap the vest onto the shirt.

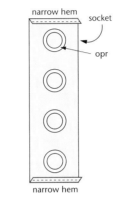

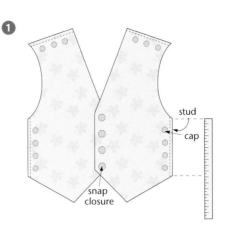

Tip:

To stabilize the shirt, use a color-coordinating quilt fabric or pre-folded bias binding larger than the snaps. Use a zipper foot to attach the fabric to the shirt. Experiment first on scrap fabric to get the right width of fabric.

The Games We Snap

Games aren't just for kids! Here are two ideas modeled after popular children's games—Tic-Tac-Snap and Snap Four. Use your imagination to invent other great games that can be made in a snap, such as Checkers, Backgammon and more. Roll the games up and secure with a Snap Strip and the games become portable—perfect for vacations or long car trips.

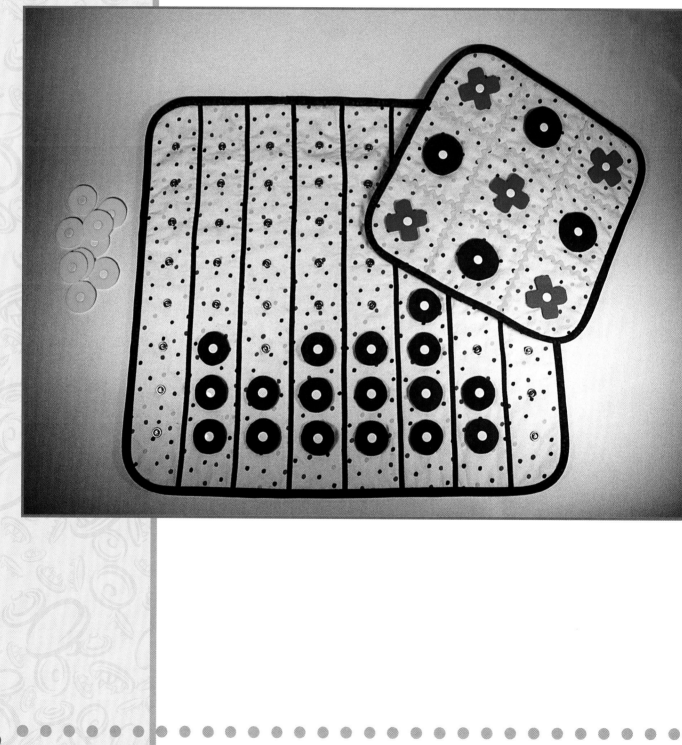

Tic-Tac-Snap

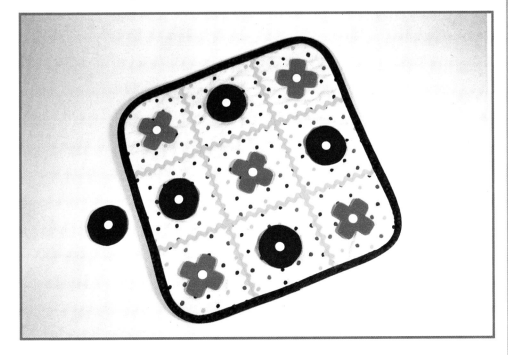

What you will need:

Fashion fabric
Batting
Binding fabric
Craft foam
Narrow ribbon
Matching thread
Marking Utensil
12 sets of prong-
   style snaps
Snap attaching tool

1 Cut two 12″ x 12″ squares of fashion fabric and one 12″ x 12″ square of batting. Layer the squares as follows, matching cut edges.

2 Center, pin and stitch ribbon 4″ apart to create the cross-hatches of the game.

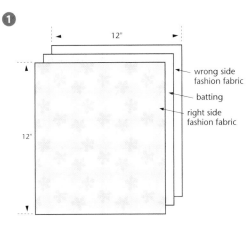

wrong side
fashion fabric

batting

right side
fashion fabric

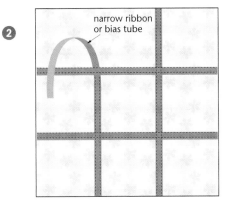

narrow ribbon
or bias tube

3 Slightly round the corners for ease in adding binding.

4 Attach snaps according to manufacturer's instructions in the center of each square. Be sure to use the correct snap components as illustrated. Using your favorite quilt binding method, stitch a binding around the square to seal raw edges. (Consult your favorite quilting instructional book for details.)

5 Trace and cut five each of the 'x' and 'o' templates. Attach snaps according to manufacturer's instructions. Be sure to use the correct snap components as illustrated.

3

Slightly round corners

4

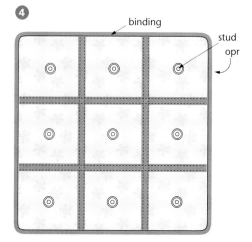

binding

stud
opr

5

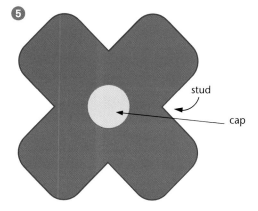

stud

cap

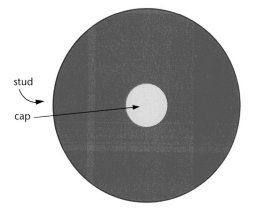

stud

cap

Snap Four

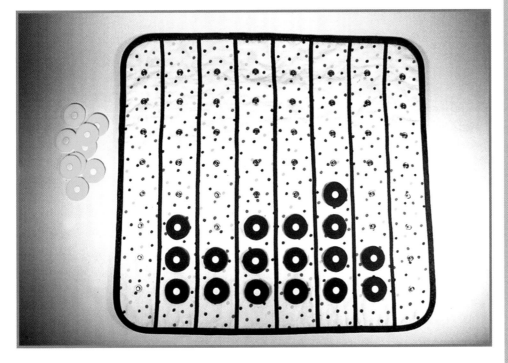

What you will need:

Fashion fabric
Batting
Binding fabric
Marking instrument
Craft foam
Narrow ribbon
Snap Strip
  (See page 75)
Matching thread
64 Sets of
  prong-style snaps
Snap attaching tool

Cut one rectangle 20-1/2" x 19" inches long from the fashion fabric for the back of the game. Cut one square of batting 20-1/2" wide x 19" long.

1 For the pieced top of the game, cut eight strips 19" long by 3" wide. Mark the fabric strips every 2" starting 2-1/2" from the top of each strip. This will determine where snaps will be set onto fabric. Attach snaps according to the manufacturer's instructions. Be sure to use the correct snap components as illustrated.

2 After snaps are set, sew strips using a 1/4" seam allowance with right sides together. Finger press the seams flat.

1

3"

19"

stud

opr

2

3 Layer the squares as shown, matching cut edges.

4 Slightly round the corners for ease in adding binding.

5 Pin and stitch ribbon through all layers over the seams of the pieced game top.

6 Using your favorite quilt binding method, stitch a binding around the square to seal the raw edges. (Consult you favorite quilting instructional book for details.)

7 Trace and cut 64 circles from craft foam using the template below. Attach snaps according to manufacturer's instructions. Be sure to use the correct snap components as illustrated.

The first person to get four in a row of one color, wins!

3

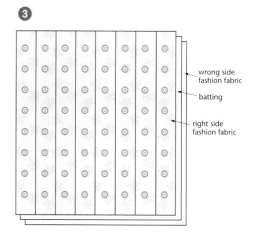

wrong side
fashion fabric

batting

right side
fashion fabric

4

Slightly
round
corners

5

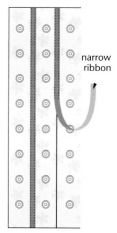

narrow
ribbon

7

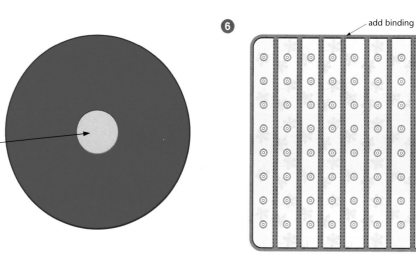

stud

cap

6

add binding

Making a Snap Strip

In an effort to make the games travel worthy, create a Snap Strip the measurement around the length of the project. To do so, cut a 1" strip of heavyweight twill tape the desired length plus 1/2" for the hems. Finish both cut edges with a narrow 1/4" inch hem.

1 To make a snap strip from coordinating quilt cotton, cut a rectangle 4" wide by the desired length plus 1/2". Fold the 4" wide strip in half and press. Tuck and press the lengthwise raw edges inside toward the wrong side of the fabric. The fabric piece should be 1" wide. See illustration #1.

Temporarily fold the fabric outward on the first fold line and stitch the two small widthwise raw edges using a 1/4" seam allowance. Turn and press; then topstitch the long (lengthwise) folds together.

2 Attach snaps according to manufacturer's instructions. Be sure to use the correct snap components as illustrated.

3 Sew one to two Snap Strips onto the wrong side of the finished game along one edge.

4 Roll up, snap and you'll be on your way!

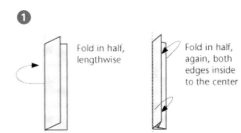

1 Fold in half, lengthwise

Fold in half, again, both edges inside to the center

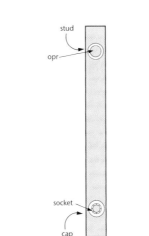

2 stud
opr
socket
cap

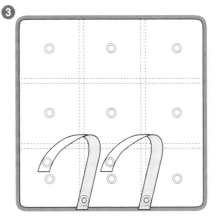

3

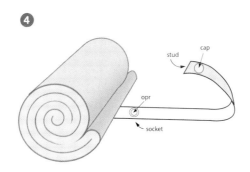

4 stud cap
opr
socket

What you will need:

Coordinating, woven quilt cotton or twill tape
One prong style snap set
Snap attaching tool

Snap-It-Up Baby

Snaps are perfect for babies. In addition to making diaper changing quick, here are some ideas that make caring for babies just a little easier.

Baby Blanket Snap Up

Whether it is a purchased blanket or one created especially for baby, this handy blanket doubles as a bunting. New and experienced parents will find this idea a helpful addition to the nursery.

What you will need:

Purchased blanket with binding or Specially created blanket with binding
17 sets of long prong-style snaps
Marking utensil
Snap attaching tool

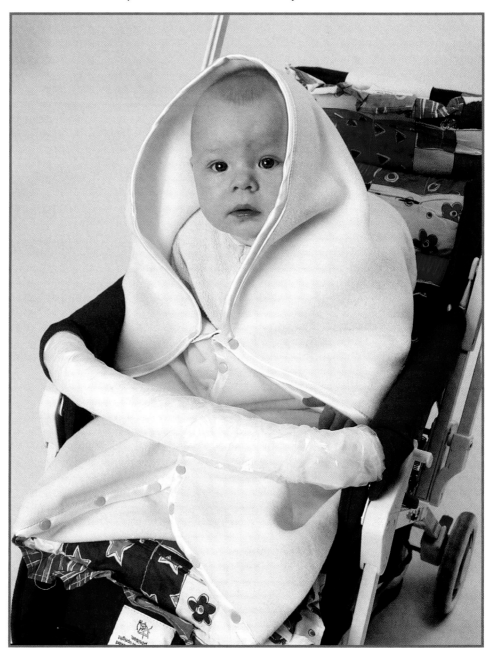

1 Purchase or create a blanket with a stable binding approximately 33" wide x 40" long. Mark the fabric where snaps are to be set onto the blanket as illustrated. Attach the snaps according to the manufacturer's instructions. Be sure to use the correct snap components as illustrated. Adjust snaps according to the size of the blanket.

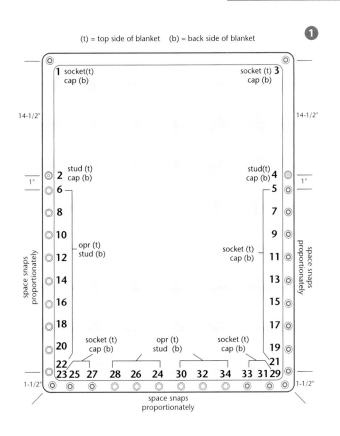

(t) = top side of blanket   (b) = back side of blanket

1

1 socket(t) cap (b)   socket (t) 3 cap (b)

14-1/2"   14-1/2"

1"   2 stud (t) cap (b)   stud(t) cap (b) 4   1"

6   5

8   7

10   9

opr (t) stud (b) 12   socket (t) cap (b) 11

14   13

16   15

18   17

20   19

22   21

space snaps proportionately   space snaps proportionately

socket (t) cap (b)   opr (t) stud (b)   socket (t) cap (b)

1-1/2" 23 25 27 28 26 24 30 32 34 33 31 29   1-1/2"

space snaps proportionately

2 To use the blanket as a bunting, refer to the numbers in illustration #1:
- Lay baby on blanket, place head in center at top.
- Fold top left and top right down, snap 1 to 2, 3 to 4.
- Fold left side and right side to meet in middle.
- Starting at 5, snap 5 to 6, 7 to 8, and 9 to 10, etc.

2

Pacifier Holder

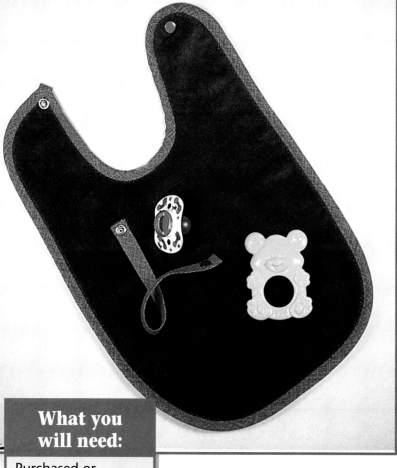

1 Stitch a Snap Strip (see page 75 for instructions) the desired length onto the bib. Be sure it is only long enough to snap and reach the child's mouth.

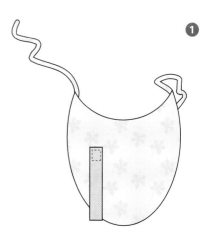

2 Attach snaps according to the manufacturer's instructions. Be sure to use the correct snap components as illustrated.

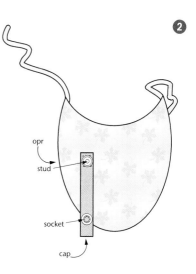

opr
stud
socket
cap

What you will need:

Purchased or
  specially made bib
Twill tape or
  matching finished
  Snap Strip
Matching thread
Prong-style snaps
Snap attaching tool

3 Slide a pacifier onto the Snap Strip and snap into place. This is also a great way to hold toys for traveling.

Detachable Bib

Here's a quick and easy project for those hard-to-handle tie-on bibs. Just add some snaps and you'll have a bib that stays with baby! It's even perfect for babies that "drool" all the time--the bib protector!

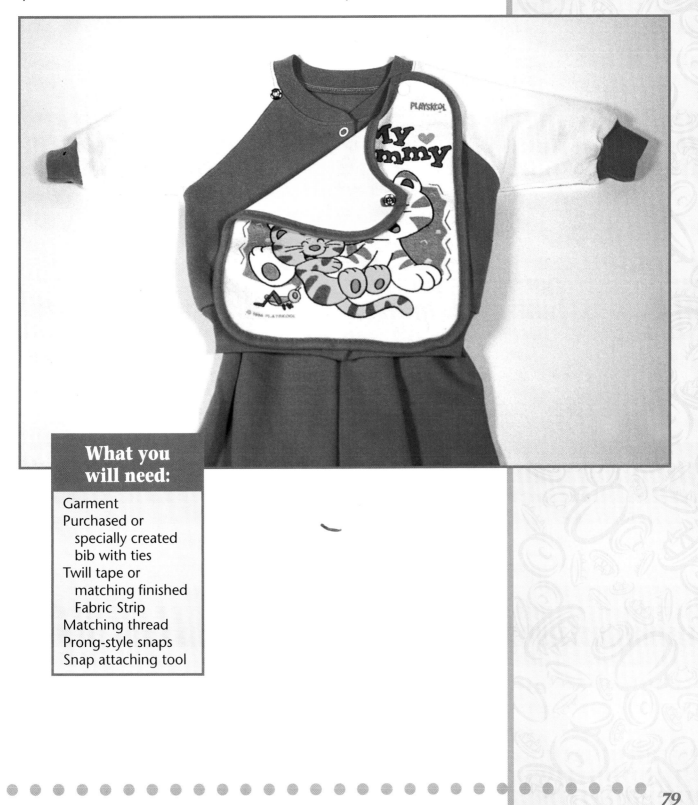

What you will need:

Garment
Purchased or
  specially created
  bib with ties
Twill tape or
  matching finished
  Fabric Strip
Matching thread
Prong-style snaps
Snap attaching tool

❶ Turn bib ties to the back side of the bib

❷ Attach snaps to the bib through all layers according to the manufacturer's instructions. Be sure to use the correct snap components as illustrated. Trim ties close to stud.

❸ Align the bib onto the garment and mark the location where snaps are to be set. Cut a 1″ x 1″ square of tricot fusible interfacing. Place the non-fusible side of the interfacing over the non-colored prong points of the snap. Once the snap is attached, fuse the interfacing onto the fabric. This will secure the snap into place without harming the fabric.

❹ Attach snaps onto the garment according to the manufacturer's instructions. Be sure to use the correct snap components as illustrated.

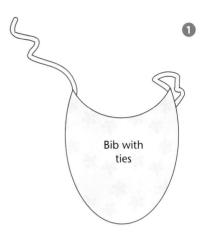

Bib with ties

❶

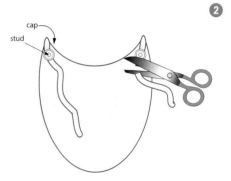

cap
stud

❷

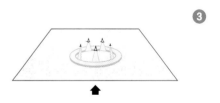

❸

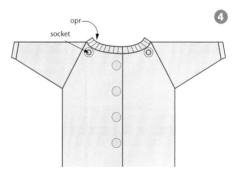

opr
socket

❹

Onesie Snap Extender

When babies outgrow onesies (a t-shirt that snaps opens and closes in the diaper-opening, and sometimes shoulder, area), it usually still fits the child everywhere *but* the diaper-opening area. In order to extend the life of a onesie, simply create a Onesie Snap Extender.

What you will need:

Coordinating woven
  or knit fabric
Woven, non-fusible
  interfacing
Prong-style snaps
Matching thread
Hand sewing needle

When customizing a Onesie Snap Extender for a purchased garment, be sure to check the snap compatibility of the onesie with the snaps attached to the extender. If the snaps are not compatible, the snaps on the onesie need to be removed and replaced with snaps identical to those used on the extender.

1 Measure the diaper opening of the onesie. Cut two rectangles the length of the diaper opening plus 1/2" wide (for seam allowances), by 3-1/2" long.

2 Cut two strips of interfacing 1" x the length of the extender. Interface one rectangle of fabric and baste or fuse the interfacing to the top and bottom of the extender as illustrated.

3 With right sides together, stitch the two extender pieces using a 1/4" seam allowance. Be sure to leave an opening for turning, then trim the corners.

4 Turn right side out, hand stitch the opening closed and press flat.

5 Attach the snaps onto the extender according to the manufacturer's instructions. Be sure to use the same brand of snaps used on the onesie, the same number of snaps and the correct snap components as illustrated.

Tip:

When sewing a onesie, consider making a coordinating Onesie Snap Extender while sewing the garment.

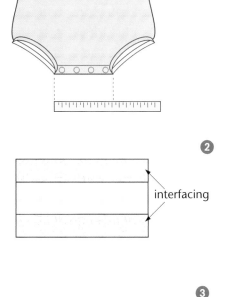

1

2

interfacing

leave an opening

3

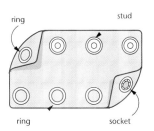

4

5

ring   stud

ring   socket

Mitten Holder

Here's a great way to keep hold of mittens for just about anyone, especially children who have a tendency to lose them.

❶ Measure the length of the jacket from cuff to cuff. Add 10" to the measurement (5" on both sides). This will be the size of the shoelace to be purchased.

❷ Knot the ends of the shoelace and attach the snaps according to the manufacturers' instructions to the mittens and shoelace as illustrated. Be sure to use the correct snap components as illustrated. Snap the mittens onto the shoelace and insert the Mitten Holder into the jacket. No more lost mittens!

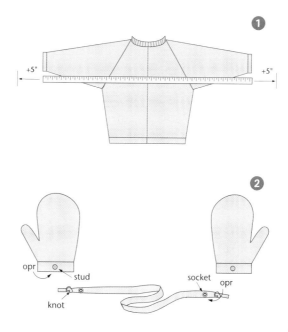

<table>
<tr><td>**What you will need:**</td></tr>
</table>

Wide shoelace
2 sets of prong-style snaps
Snap attaching tool
Mittens

More Fun with Snaps

Here's a gallery of ideas that will continue to inspire you to create easy projects perfect for kids. The companies and people who helped make these projects possible are listed and information on how to purchase the patterns can be found in the References section on page 152.

All garments shown on pages 84 and 85 are
created from patterns designed by Kwik Sew®
Pattern Co.

Here are some great ideas for kids from companies who inspire us:
1. Kwik Sew Pattern Co.
2. SJR Sew with Class
3. Sew Baby!
4. Sew Baby!
5. Kwik Sew Pattern Co.
6. Kwik Sew Pattern Co.
7. Kwik Sew Pattern Co.
8. Sew Baby !

Adults Snap It Up, Too!

Snaps aren't just for kids—snaps can go anywhere a button can without a needle and thread! Here's a look at some fun, creative ideas that'll inspire you to start snapping up adult clothing from casual to western wear.

Pictured: Nurses, doctors and medical staff benefit from using snaps on their uniforms. For heavily laundered scrubs, try stainles steel snap components. Don't forget: Hairdressers use snaps, too!

Patterns and kits from Scrubs-Buy-Mail

LEFT: Replace buttonhole closures with easy designer details and a snap. Here's how: To cover the buttonhole on the outside of the jacket, cut a geometric shape from UltraSuede® larger than the buttonhole. To cover the buttonhole area on the inside of the jacket, cut a piece of UltraSuede larger than the shape cut for the front of the jacket. Fuse the front UltraSuede piece over the buttonhole on the front of the jacket; be sure to cover the buttonhole. Use a fabric glue stick to adhere the remaining piece of Ultra-Suede to the inside buttonhole area; be sure to cover the buttonhole. On the outside of the jacket, stitch the UltraSuede piece close to the edges through all layers. Trim the excess fabric close to stitching on the inside of the jacket. Remove the button on the opposite side of the jacket. Attach snaps according to manufacturer's instructions.

Purchased jacket embellished with Ultra-Suede scraps

RIGHT: It's fun to decorate western attire with textured fabric, beads, and pearl snaps. Looking for the perfect color Pearl Snap to match your art-to-wear project? Consider dying white Pearl Snaps the color you are looking for. To do so, use a craft dye specially formulated for synthetic material (see page 54 for more information). Instructions on how to texturize fabric can be found in Linda McGehee's book titled *Creating Texture With Textiles* from Krause Publications.

Garment created by Jan Hutto

Reversible snaps are the perfect closure for vests. Put your time into creating one garment with two different designs—one inside and one outside! For more on reversible closures, see page 17. As shown, crazy quilt one side of a vest and show-off gorgeous batik fabric on the other.

Garment created by Jan Hutto
Pattern from Kwik Sew Pattern
Company

Rugby-style necklines made from polar-type fabrics are best made with lighter-weight woven facings. This is just one of several ways to eliminate the bulk of a garment. The facing can be created from a lightweight twill (as shown) or wind-breaker fabric. This application is perfect for post or prong style snaps depending on the thickness of fabric. Be sure to sew a machine eyelet at the location the post-style snaps will be set. This step eliminates the strain fabric endures with a post-style snap closure (see page 29 for more information).

Garment and pattern designed by Kwik Sew Pattern Company

Wind-breaker fabric, such as Supplex®, is perfect for any style jacket and post-style snaps. Supplex and similar fabrics are considered densely woven fabrics. When attaching prong-style snaps to this type of material, puckering of the fabric surrounding the snap may occur (see page 26 for more information). This is why post-style snaps are recommended for these fabric types.

Garment and pattern designed by Kwik Sew Pattern Company

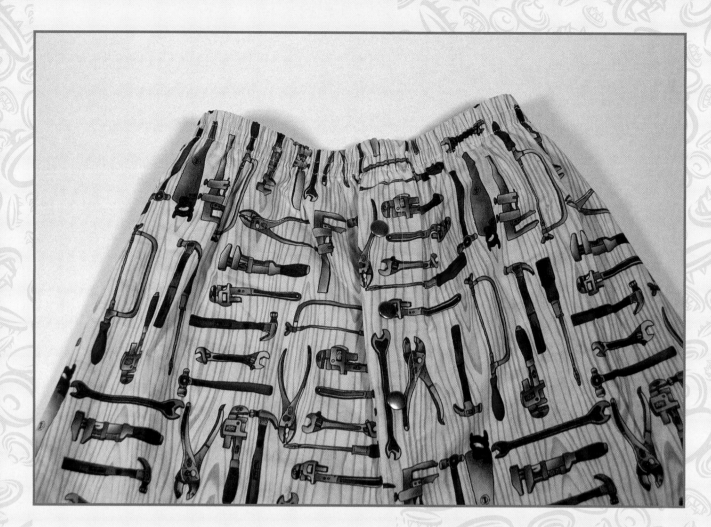

Above: Let's not forget the men in our lives! Surprise him with a pair of boxer shorts using snaps as the closure instead of buttons.

Shorts created by Jeanine Twigg
Patterns from Kwik Sew Pattern Company

Right: Consider using snaps for the closure of wool projects. Interface loosely woven wool with a tricot fusible interfacing (shown) and attach long-prong style snaps. Interface thick, dense wool with a woven, non-fusible interfacing and attach post-style snaps.

Garment created by Jeanine Twigg
Pattern from Kwik Sew Pattern Company

Create some fun, embroidered "snap-art" with the Snap It Up! Embroidery Disk from Cactus Punch. As shown, cover a buttonhole or embroider a design on the placket of a shirt. Let the embroidery program pre-determine the location where the snap should to be placed. Use color-coordinating threads and snaps to create an original piece of "snap-art"! (Note: This technique is for owners of embroidery equipment.)

Embellishment by Jeanine Twigg
Purchased tuxedo shirt

Embellish a jeans vest with color-coordinating Pearl Snaps and designer fabrics. The perfect application for western wear detailing.

Garment and pattern from Kwik Sew Pattern Company

This project is super simple and can be made in a snap! Simply cut geometric shapes from Ultrasuede and snap 'em onto a garment using the fashion-colored snap top and socket. Be sure the reach of your snap attaching tool will allow you to attach snaps in the middle of a garment or project.

Garment created by Jeanine Twigg

Left: Using snaps for decoration instead of function can lead to many designer details. By using only a portion of the snap set (the fashion-colored snap top and the socket), you can utilize snaps as decorative studs. Try stitching cotton braiding onto a vest (shown) in a "stippling" pattern. Attach snaps in several different sizes as design elements. Be sure to pre-shrink the cotton braiding as you would twill tape (instructions for pre-shrinking twill tape are found on page 28). Be sure the reach of your snap attaching tool will allow you to attach snaps to the middle of a garment or project.

Garment created by Jeanine Twigg
Pattern from Kwik Sew Pattern Company

Right: Try making a typical men's shirt unique by adding decorative Pearl Snaps.

Shirt created by Kwik Sew Pattern Company
Patterns from Kwik Sew Pattern Company

Design western attire with decorative threads and snaps to match. Use a double needle threaded with silver and gold metallic thread to stitch the detailing. Then, snap up the shirt with alternating white pearl snaps with a silver rim and with a gold rim. This designer detail will add to western-wear fun!

Garment created by Jan Hutto

Polar-type fabrics and long-prong snaps are perfect for each other. By eliminating the facing bulk when sewing this luxurious fabric, garments will lay attractively against the body when worn. See page 44 for more information on how to remove the bulk from a garment. Cotton quilt fabric is all you need to help you achieve the bulk-less facing.

Garment created by Jeanine Twigg
Pattern from Kwik Sew Pattern Company

Snaps make a great pocket embellishment. This versatile vest is perfect for embellishing with post-style snaps. The vest is designed for hunting and fishing, but ladies, this vest is perfect for power-shopping, too!

Garment and pattern designed by Kwik Sew Pattern Company

Quilting and no-sew snaps are the perfect combination. Choose a fun quilted jacket pattern that calls for buttons and use easy-to-attach snaps instead! With the wide range of colored snaps available, consider color-coordinating your snaps to the garment quilt fabric.

Garment created by Jeanine Twigg

Also use wind-breaker fabric to surround polar-type fabrics before setting post-style snaps (as shown). The added support of the wind-breaker fabric will prevent the snap from pulling out of the garment . In addition, this designer detail will eliminate the step of making a machine eyelet before pre-punching a hole in the fabric. Color-coordinating quilt-cotton can also be used to add some color to a solid polar-type fabric.

Garment and pattern designed by Kwik Sew Pattern Company

This designer thread detail is a snap! Appliqué geometric shapes onto the front of a vest (pictured) or jacket using a decorative machine stitch. Next, determine the length of thread you will need—add about two inches per appliqué for the thread ease. Choose four to six coordinating thread strands for the project. Starting at a seam with all thread strands together, stitch the threads to the seam allowance. Pull the threads to be sure they are securely attached to the garment. Loosely, glide the threads to the first appliqué — be sure to give a couple inches of ease for the loose, decorative detail. Stitch the threads to the center of the appliqué. Pull the threads to be sure they are securely attached to the garment. Finish securing the remaining thread to the appliqués until all the thread has been used. Attach a fashion-colored, long-prong snap and socket to each appliqué directly over stitching. There is no need to use the stud and open prong ring for this project.

*Garment created by
Jeanine Twigg
Pattern from Kwik Sew
Pattern Company*

An elegant basic black dress closed
with snaps? You bet! Embellish any
elegant outfit with silver and gold
snaps (as shown) close together as a
closure. One snap functions and the
other is used for decoration. Use only
the fashion-colored snap top and
socket for the decorative portion of the
closure.

Garment created by Jeanine Twigg
Pattern from Kwik Sew Pattern Company

Snaps make the perfect accent for any style of home decor. It's easy to snap up everything from pillows to soft, cozy blankets. Simply look around your home to see where you can add a little snap to your decor!

Home Dec in a Snap

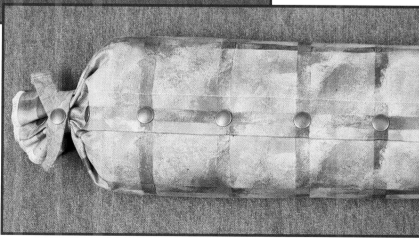

Snap Easy Pillows

Everyone loves pillows! They come in all shapes, sizes and styles. And, pillows can be made quickly—especially when snaps are the finishing detail!

What you will need:

Fabric of choice
such as:
Polar-type, home
dec or quilt
cotton
Matching thread
Woven non-fusible
interfacing
Marking utensil
Prong-style snaps
Snap attaching tool
Snap Strip
(See page 75)
Pillow forms or
blankets/towels

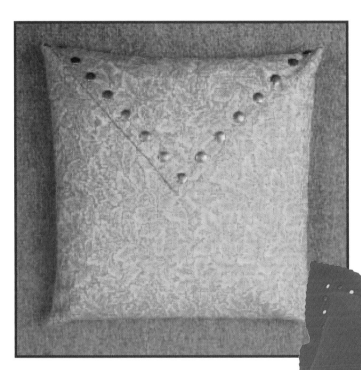

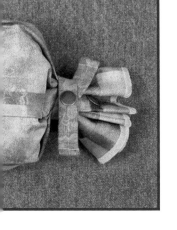

Snap Shams

Snap Shams are perfect for storing extra bed pillows. Consider using complimentary or left-over fabric from the Comforter Cover (See page 118).

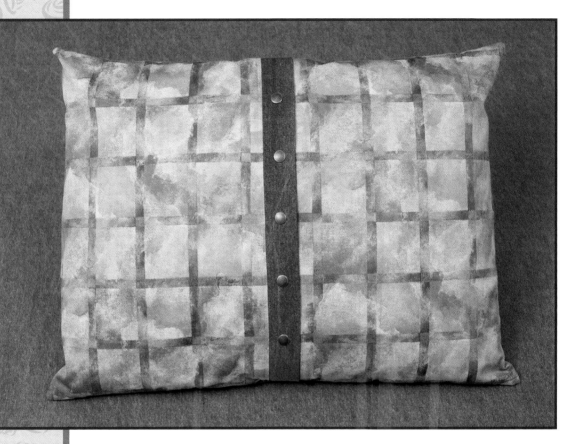

❶ To determine the size needed to create the Snap Shams, measure around bed pillows in length (A) and width (B). Divide each of these measurements by two.

❷ For the back of the Snap Sham, cut one rectangle the determined length (plus 1") and width (plus 1") of the measurement above. For the front of the Snap Sham, cut one rectangle an extra 7" in width than the back.

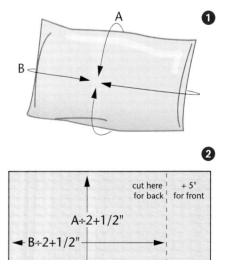

❶

A

B

❷

cut here | + 5"
for back | for front

A÷2+1/2"

◄ B÷2+1/2" ►

❸ Cut the front in half lengthwise. Cut two interfacing strips the determined length of the front by 1-1/2" wide. On the wrong side of the fabric, align the interfacing strips to the cut's edge and overcast the raw edges. Fold the facings toward the wrong side, press and topstitch down.

❹ Attach snaps according to manufacturer's instructions 3/4" from fold line. Be sure to use the correct snap components as illustrated.

❺ Snap the front closed.

❻ With right sides together, lay the back over the front and stitch with a 1/4" seam allowance on all four sides and trim the corners. (For a decorator accent, insert cording or a ruffle here.)

❼ Unsnap the front and turn the sham right side out. Insert bed pillow through snap opening and snap cover closed.

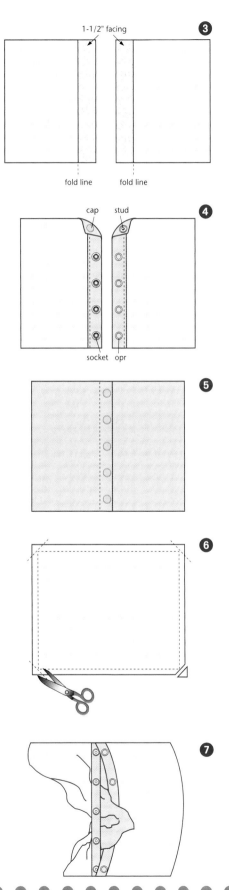

Tip:

If fabric is thick or colorful and you want the snaps to stand out, consider adding a decorative coordinating band, as pictured. Cut a 4" strip of fabric, fold in half and stitch to each raw edge. Interface if necessary.

Blanket Roll

A Blanket Roll is a great place to store not only sheet blankets but beach towels. For a lightweight option, use a roll of batting in place of a blanket.

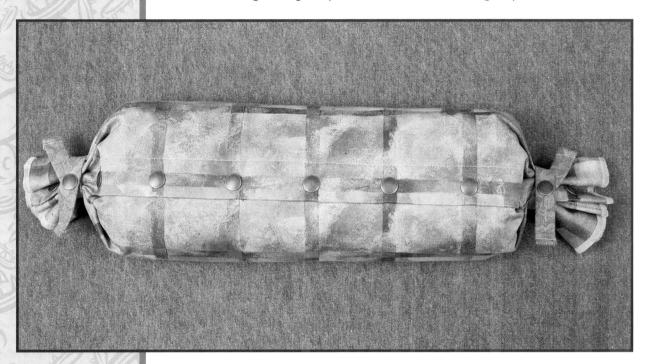

❶ Fold a blanket in half and again in thirds.

❷ Roll the blanket tightly. To determine the size needed to create the Blanket Roll, measure around the roll in length (A) and width (B). Divide the width (B) measurement by two.

❶

Fold blanket

❷

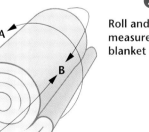

Roll and measure blanket

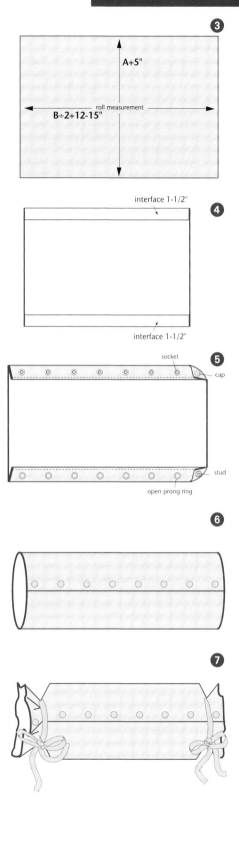

3 Cut the decorator fabric the determined measurement of the width (B) plus 12" to 15" (depending on the size of the blanket) by the measurement of the length (A) plus 5".

4 Cut two interfacing strips the determined length of the front cut edges by 1-1/2" wide. On the wrong side of the fabric, align the interfacing strips to the cut edges and overcast the raw edges.

5 Fold the facings toward the wrong side, press and topstitch down. Attach snaps according to manufacturer's instructions 3/4" from the fold line. Be sure to use the correct snap components as illustrated.

6 On the inside of the Blanket Roll, lay the rolled object in the center lengthwise. Snap the roll closed.

7 Secure the ends of the roll with ribbon or a Snap Strip (See page 75).

Snapelope

This Envelope Pillow makes a great accent for either a bed or couch. If the Snapelope is made smaller, it makes a great purse. Simply make it from leather, add a long chain and you'll have a fun, sporty purse!

❶ Determine the size of the square pillow form. Cut one rectangle of fabric equal to 3 times the length of the pillow form by the width of the pillow form plus 1/2" for the seam allowances. Mark fold lines on the wrong side of the fabric. Finish one short end of the rectangle. Fold and press the two short ends toward the wrong side of the fabric one-half the length of the pillow form.

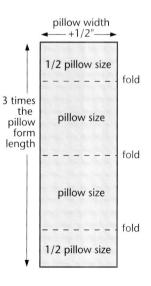

❶

2 To make the triangular flap, unfold the rectangle and fold in half lengthwise with right sides together. Matching cut edges, stitch a 1/4″ seam allowance on the unfinished edge of the rectangle and trim the corner.

3 Turn the stitched seam to the right side and re-fold to form the triangular flap. Overcast all raw edges and press. Re-fold the other end of the rectangle toward the wrong side.

4 With right sides together, fold the rectangle on the remaining fold line to form the square.

5 Stitch the sides with 1/4″ seam allowance.

6 Turn right sides out and press.

7 Attach the fashion colored snap top and sockets according to the manufacturer's instructions. Be sure to use the correct snap components as illustrated. Insert pillow form to determine the placement of the stud and the open ring. Remove the pillow form and attach the remaining components according to the manufacturer's instructions. Be sure to use the correct snap components as illustrated. Only one snap functions—the one at the end of the triangle—and the remaining snaps are for decoration.

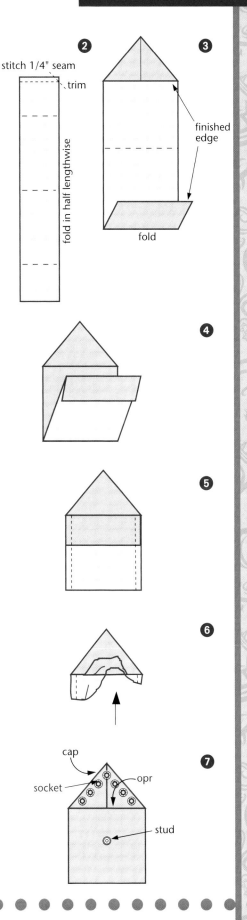

No-Sew Simple Snapillow

Create this pillow out of a super-sized pillow form and polar-type fabric. Add lots of reversible snaps and you'll have a fun pillow for the family room.

Tip:

Use a ready-made foam pillow to give this pillow more stability. In addition, interface the triangle shape for added strength.

❶ Cut two pieces of polar-type fabric the size of the pillow form plus 2-1/2" on all sides. Attach reversible snap sets according to the manufacturer's instructions. Set one snap in each corner and evenly space the remaining snaps. It's recommended to space snaps about 1-1/2" apart. Be sure to use the correct snap components as illustrated.

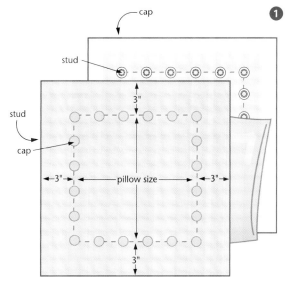

Sew Easy Pillow Cover

Here's another great idea for use with polar-type fabrics. Decorate one or both sides with embroidery, appliqué or make a collection of seasonal covers.

Tip:

To save yourself a step, make the cover from a ready-made dish towel. Appliqué the towel, stitch ends together, apply snaps, insert pillow and you'll have a great gift for any occasion.

❶ Determine the size of the pillow form. Cut one piece of fabric equal to 2 times the length of the pillow form plus 1" for seam allowances by the width of the pillow form plus 9". Fold the fabric piece lengthwise with right sides together and match cut edges.

❷ Stitch the length of the fabric with 1/4" seam allowance. Overcast the raw edges, press a 1" hem and topstitch.

❸ Turn the pillow cover right side out. Attach reversible snap sets according to the manufacturer's instructions 3-1/2" in from the opening on both sides. Be sure to use the correct snap components as illustrated.

❶

fold

❷

❸

reversible closure

caps outside

socket/stud inside

Super Saver Comforter Cover

Have you ever had to climb into a duvet cover to smooth out the comforter? Well, climb out of the cover and try this innovative design that aids with the comforter insertion and adds to the decor of any bedroom. With denim being the fabric of choice for garments, why not take denim into the bedroom for a look that's classic. Best of all, there's no seaming of the decorator fabric for the top!

What you will need:

Fabric of choice such as:
Washable home-dec fabrics 54" to 60" wide
Matching thread
Jeans Topstitching thread (optional)
Woven non-fusible interfacing
Marking Utensil
Long prong-style snaps
Snap attaching tool

❶ With the comforter on the bed, measure the length (A) and the width (B) of the comforter as illustrated.

2 For the back of the Comforter Cover, cut one rectangle of backing material the determined length (A) plus 1/2" for seam allowances and width (B) plus 1/2" for seam allowances. Seam backing material if necessary to achieve the finished size.

3 For the front of the Comforter Cover, cut two lengths of 54" to 60" wide decorator fabric the determined length (A) plus 1/2" for seam allowances. Depending on the size of the bed, trim the 60" wide fabric to 54". Use the remnants for tabs on curtains. Cut four interfacing strips the determined length (A) of the front by 1-1/2" wide. On the wrong side of the fabric, align the interfacing strips to the selvage edge of the fabric and overcast the edges to secure the interfacing.

4 Fold the facing toward the wrong side, press and topstitch down. On one of the two lengths of fabric, attach the fashion colored caps and the sockets according to manufacturer's instructions 3/4" from fold line on both lengthwise finished edges. Be sure to use the correct snap components as illustrated. It's recommended to attach snaps at least 2" apart and starting 2-1/2" from the top and bottom.

5 Fold the other finished length of fabric in half lengthwise with right sides together. Press and cut the piece in two on the fold using the press edge as a guide.

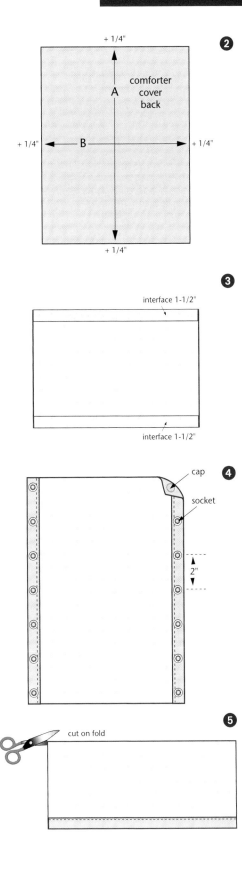

2 +1/4"

comforter cover back

A

+1/4" ◄— B —► +1/4"

+1/4"

3

interface 1-1/2"

interface 1-1/2"

4 cap socket 2"

5 cut on fold

Tip:

Trim the backing fabric smaller than the pieced top (1/2" to 1" on all sides). This will prevent the backing fabric from showing when the Comforter Cover is on the bed.

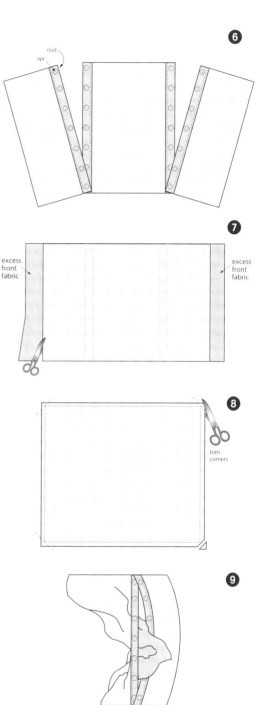

To prevent shifting of the comforter inside the cover, insert snap tabs inside the cover before stitching seam allowances. Attach the stud and open ring to the snap tab and attach the socket and open ring to the comforter edge using manufacturer's instructions.

6 Working on a large flat surface, lay the whole, snapped front section on the surface with the right side down. Align the facings of the two front pieces with the facings of the whole front section, as illustrated. Determine where the remaining snap components are to be set and mark fabric. Attach the studs and open rings according to manufacturer's instructions 3/4" from fold line. Be sure to use the correct snap components as illustrated.

7 Snap all the finished pieces of the Comforter Cover front together. With right sides together and matching raw edges, center the backing fabric over the snapped front. Be sure the same amount of extra fabric is on both sides of the backing fabric. Trim off the excess fabric from the Comforter Cover front—reserve this fabric for making the Snap Shams or accent pillow for the bed. (Note: This would be a good time to attach snaps to the backing fabric for the Detachable Bed Border (see page 123). Be sure the studs are attached to the outside of the fabric.

8 With right sides together, pin and stitch the front and back sections together with a 1/4" seam allowance; trim corners.

9 Unsnap comforter cover and turn right sides out, then snap closed.

To insert the comforter into the Comforter Cover, lay the Comforter Cover on the bed in the finished position. Completely unsnap the cover on both sides of the bed. Feed the comforter under the snapped section of the cover until it is smooth on both sides of the bed and the sides of the comforter are still exposed. Tuck the exposed sides of the comforter in the cover and snap it closed. For another fun look, use the above instructions to create one closure down the middle of the bed.

Detachable Bed Border

Here's a fun quilt project that requires half the time of a full bed quilt. What's more, it's detachable! Snap the Bed Border to the Comforter Cover and you'll have a creative accent that can easily be changed as styles or decorator tastes come and go. Choose from two border lengths—under the pillow accent or over the bed pillow for quick and easy bed making.

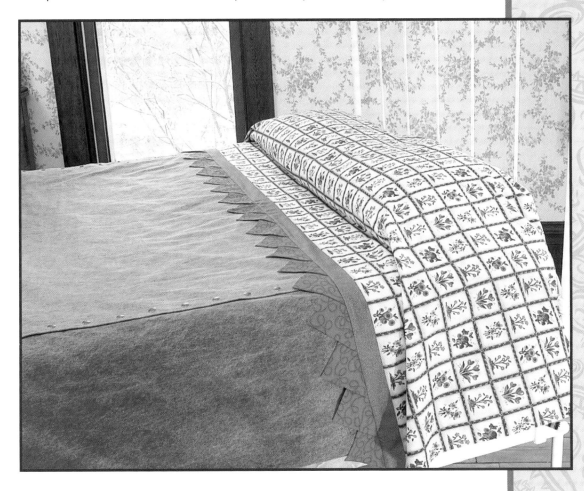

What you will need:

Quilt cottons
Quilt design of choice
Matching thread
Woven non-fusible interfacing
Marking Utensil
Prong-style snaps
Snap attaching tool

Tip:

If you are planning to attach the Detachable Bed Border to the Super Saver Comforter Cover, see page 120 for construction details and snap placement.

❶ Measure the width of the comforter (B) to determine how wide to make the Detachable Bed Border. For the "under-the-pillow" border, measure from the top edge of the comforter to the desired length. For the "over-the-pillow" border, measure from the top edge of the comforter, under the pillow, up and over the pillow and to the desired length.

❷ Using a favorite quilt pattern or design, create a pieced top the determined length plus 1/2" for seam allowances by the determined width plus 1/2" for seam allowances. Once the pieced top has been completed, cut a backing for the border the same size as the pieced top. With right sides together, stitch the backing and the pieced top together using a 1/4" seam allowance. Leave a 6" opening for turning. Turn the border to the right side and stitch opening closed (by hand); press. Attach the stud and open ring to the border according to manufacturer's instructions 3/4" from seamed edge— attach snaps at least 2" apart and starting 2" from the two sides. Be sure to use the correct snap components as illustrated.

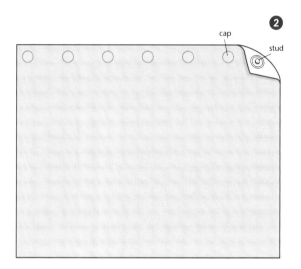

❶ Measure up and around for over pillow style — Measure here for under pillow style

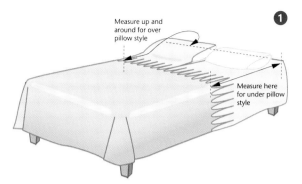

❷ cap · stud

3 On the Comforter Cover or purchased comforter, align the Detachable Bed Border with the edge of the comforter in the finished position. Determine the snap placement and mark the comforter where the snaps are to be set. Attach the fashion colored caps and the sockets according to manufacturer's instructions 3/4" from fold line. Be sure to use the correct snap components as illustrated.

4 Snap the border to the comforter as shown.

5 Flip the border to the right side of the comforter.

Tip:

For a simple look, snap on eyelet fabric or lace. Be sure to face and interface the eyelet or lace properly before attaching the snaps.

Snappy Tab Curtains

With the multitude of window treatment possibilities, Snappy Tab Curtains are sure to make decorating a window easy. Whether your window needs a valance or complete coverage, these versatile curtains adapt to any decor. Once you make one, you'll be snapping up your whole home from shower tab curtains to closet tab curtains.

What you will need:

Fabric of choice such as:
  Home dec or quilt
  cotton
Woven non-fusible
  interfacing
Matching Thread
Marking utensil
Prong-style snaps
Snap attaching tool

1 To determine the finished size of the curtains, measure the inside (or outside) of the window or wherever the curtain will be hanged. Cut the decorator fabric twice this measurement width plus 3" for hems by the desired length plus 4" for hems and tab allowance (4"). Adjust these measurements for personal preference on tab allowances. Press and pin a double 3/4" hem on both sides of the curtain. Press and pin a double 2" hem along the base edge; topstitch through all layers.

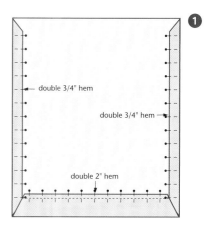

1

double 3/4" hem

double 3/4" hem

double 2" hem

2 Press and pin a double 2" hem along the top edge. Topstitch through all layers.

3 Loops should be evenly spaced 4" to 6" apart depending on personal preference. Cut two loops approximately 2-1/2"x 10" depending on the desired finished loop size. Cut the necessary amount of loops for the curtains the length of the fabric, for stability. With right sides together, stitch three sides of each loop with a 1/4" seam allowance, as shown.

4 On the folded edge of the loop, insert a yardstick into the wrong side of the loop.

5 While holding onto the seam allowance, continue moving the loop onto the yardstick until the loop is completely turned to the right side. Pull the turned loop off the yardstick and press.

6 Stitch the loops onto the back of the curtains over the previous stitching as shown. Press the loops up toward the top of the curtain.

7 Attach snaps according to manufacturer's instructions. Be sure to use the correct snap components as illustrated.

Tip:

If your fabric is bulky, consider turning up a single hem with a strip of interfacing. Alter fabric measurements if necessary.

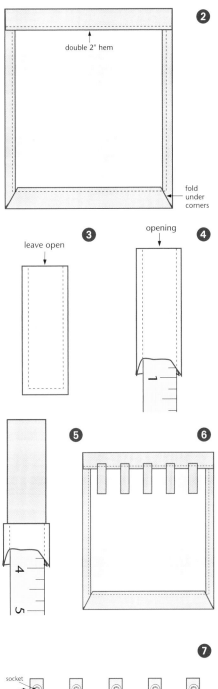

2

double 2" hem

fold under corners

3 leave open

4 opening

5

6

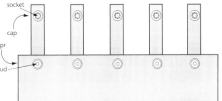

7

socket
cap
opr
stud

Tip:

If the curtains will be lined, cut the lining the same size as the finished curtain. Before top stitching the hems, unpin them, tuck the lining under the hem allowance, re-pin and topstitch through all layers.

Tip:

Polar-type fabrics also make great tab curtains for the winter months. Consider lining the polar with supplex and making the curtain the size of the window for warmth.

The Hot 'n' Cold Blanket

When it comes to sleeping arrangements, traditionally a wife is always cold and a husband is always hot. Here's a great way to solve the temperature control problems without fighting for the blankets. It's the perfect gift idea for newlyweds and will surely get a few laughs!

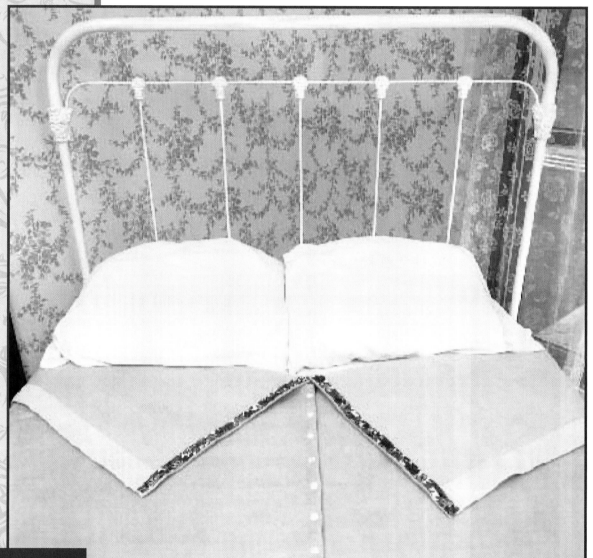

What you will need:

Polar-type fabrics or
   purchased blanket
Matching Thread
Twill tape or
   Complimentary
   woven fabric
Long-prong snaps

If you're starting from scratch, make a blanket the desired size and finish the raw edges. If you're starting with a purchased bed blanket, make sure it is oversized. Cut the blanket in two lengthwise.

❶ Cut two pieces of 1-1/2" wide twill tape or a complimentary woven fabric strip the length of the cut edge plus 1" by 3" wide. Fold the fabric strip in half lengthwise and press. Unfold the short cut edges to the wrong side and stitch with a 1/4" seam allowance. Turn to the right side and press. With right sides together and matching cut edges, stitch the twill or fabric strips to the blanket using a 1/4" seam allowance.

❷ Understitch the seam allowance to the fabric strips.

❸ Turn fabric strips to the wrong side of the blanket and topstitch down. Attach snaps according to manufacturer's instructions. Be sure to use the correct snap components as illustrated. Attach snaps at least 2" apart and starting close to the top and bottom of the blanket.

❹ Snap and unsnap the blanket as shown. Consider embroidering 'HERS' and 'HIS' for the perfect shower gift!

❺ As a variation of this blanket, create a blanket that unsnaps four ways. This idea makes a great blanket for the kids, too! Keep adding panels as they grow.

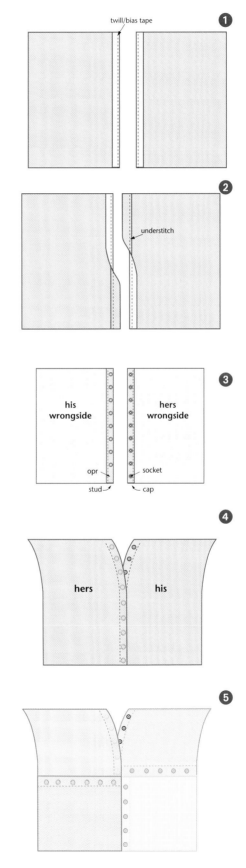

Tip:

Consider using Polarfleece® or polar-type fabric for the project. When stitching the fabric strips onto the blanket, place the blanket fabric next to the feed dogs of the sewing machine or serger. The machine will help eliminate puckering of fabrics.

One of the best and most rewarding uses of our sewing talents is to create items for those in need. Whether you're replacing buttons with snaps to make it a little easier for those with arthritic hands or sewing a pocket pouch for someone who travels with two hands, give the gift of snaps to someone who might need a little "snap-me-up!"

Snaps
for Special Needs

Buttons to Snaps

Sometimes buttons can be a challenge to pull through a buttonhole. Replace ordinary shirt buttons with colorful, easy-to-fasten snaps and end "dressing frustration."

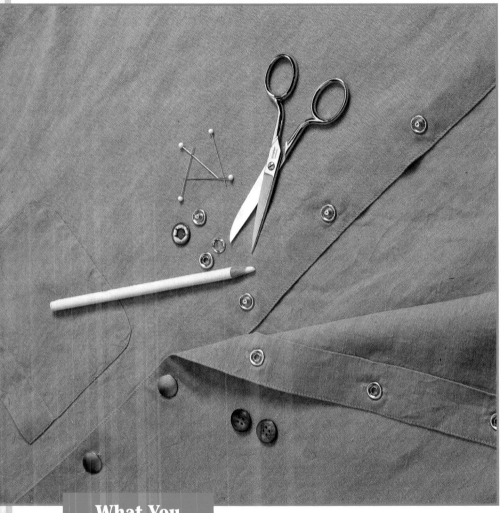

What You Will Need:

Woven quilt cotton
Scissors
Marking utensil
Prong-style snaps
Snap attaching tool

① Snip the threads carefully to remove the button. Remove the cut threads from the garment and button. Identify and mark the location where the thread was removed from the garment.

② Using the decorative snap cap, center the snap prongs directly over the buttonhole. Be sure the prongs are on both sides of the buttonhole. Attach the decorative snap cap and socket snaps according to the manufacturer's instructions. Be sure to use the correct snap components as illustrated.

③ Confirm that the location of the marks opposite the buttonhole align with the snap components attached over the buttonhole. If necessary, adjust markings accordingly. Attach the stud and open ring according to the manufacturer's instructions. Be sure to use the correct snap components as illustrated.

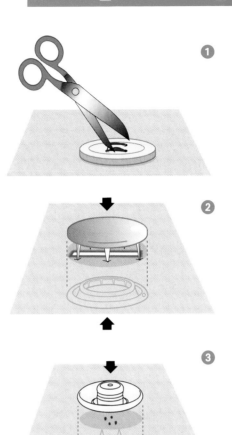

Tip:

Cover the buttonhole completely with the snap or cover only a portion of it—the snap will then look like a button. Either way, you'll have the look of button with the convenience of a snap!

Adding a Back Closure

When taking care of people with special needs, it is much easier to dress someone from the back of the body than it is from the front. Pulling garments over the head or swinging arms to the back of the body can be challenging. To make dressing easier, use this idea to add a back closure to just about any garment—especially sweatshirts.

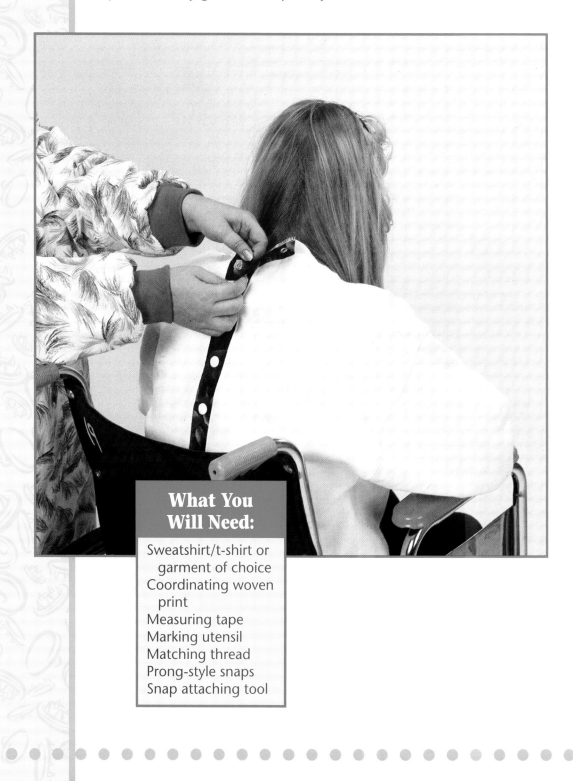

What You Will Need:

Sweatshirt/t-shirt or
  garment of choice
Coordinating woven
  print
Measuring tape
Marking utensil
Matching thread
Prong-style snaps
Snap attaching tool

Identify and mark the center back of the sweatshirt or garment of choice. Cut open the back on the marked center back—be careful not to cut through to the front of the garment. Trim off an additional 1/2" on both cut edges to ensure the snaps are set at the center back.

1 Measure the length of the cut edge. Cut two strips of fashion quilt fabric the length of the cut edge plus 1/2" for seam allowances by 6" wide.

2 Fold the strips of fabric in half lengthwise and press. Fold and press in half again lengthwise. Stitch the short end of the raw edges with a 1/4" seam allowance and turn the strip so that all wrong sides are inward.

3 With right sides together and matching cut edges, stitch the strips to the back of the sweatshirt lengthwise with a 1/4" seam allowance.

4 Press the seam allowance toward the sweatshirt and edgestitch the seam allowance to the garment.

5 Attach the snaps according to the manufacturer's instructions. Be sure to use the correct snap components as illustrated.

Tip:

This project can be for a front closure as well as a back closure. You can even make your own sweatshirt or t-shirt to show off your sewing talents.

133

Helpful Pocket Pouch

When the transportation of one's body takes both hands, how can you safeguard your belongings? Try adding a pocket to the upper front of a pant leg, or make this a pocket pouch that can be easily removed and attached to another garment.

What You Will Need:

Woven fabric
Washable woven non-fusible interfacing
Scissors
Marking utensil
Measuring tape
Matching thread
Prong-style snaps
Snap attaching tool
Zipper foot for sewing machine

❶ Cut two rectangles 8" wide by 17-1/2" long. With right sides together, stitch using a 1/4" seam allowance around all sides; leave a 4" opening for turning.

❷ Turn right sides out and topstitch close to the edges. Mark, fold and press lines.

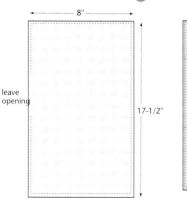

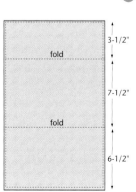

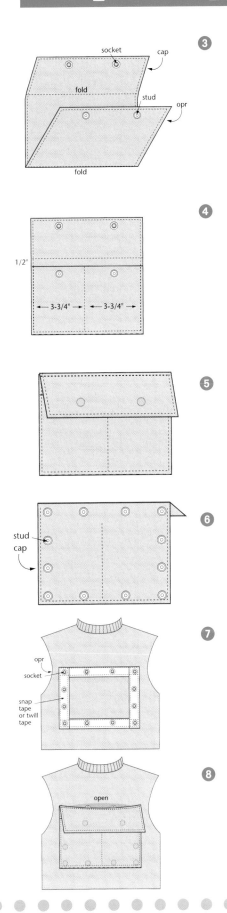

❸ Attach two sets of snaps according to the manufacturer's instructions. Be sure to use the correct snap components as illustrated.

❹ Re-fold the bottom of the rectangle to form the pouch. There will be a 1/2" space from the top flap fold line to the top edge of the pouch. Stitch over previous stitching on the sides through all layers.

❺ Re-fold the top flap of the rectangle; topstitch.

❻ For the pouch, attach four snaps on each side of the pouch according to the manufacturer's instructions. Be sure to use the correct snap components as illustrated. Attach snaps under the top flap of the pouch within the 1/2" gap or slightly under the pocket. Be careful not to catch compartment fabric in the snap.

❼ To secure the pouch to the garment, attach snaps to twill tape or matching snap strips (see page 75) in a rectangle the exact size of the pouch. Mark the location where snaps are to be set. Attach the snaps according to the manufacturer's instructions. Be sure to use the correct snap components as illustrated. Stitch using a zipper foot close to the edge. Snap tape can also be used—see Chapter 4 to learn how to make your own snap tape.

❽ Snap on and off the pouch as needed. Or, completely remove the pouch to use as a purse. It is helpful to create one pouch and many shirts to snap the pouch onto. Unsnap the middle two snaps at the top of the pouch away from garment to store larger items.

Walkin' 'n' Wheelin' Satchel

Whether walking or wheeling to where you need to go, don't forget this satchel. It's just the perfect size to carry books, newspapers or whatever it is you need on your journey.

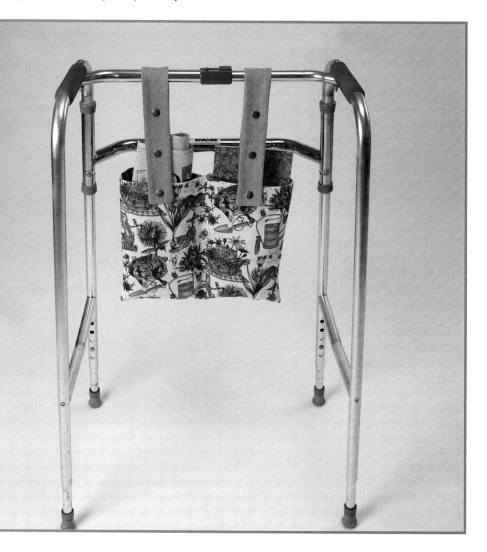

❶ Measure the walker or wheelchair base. For a standard 18" to 20" base walker or wheelchair, cut two rectangles of fabric 15" wide by 25" long. Adjust the measurement accordingly for a smaller or larger walker or wheelchair. Place the two rectangles wrong sides together. Treat the two pieces of fabric as one. Finish both 15-1/2" wide raw edges and press a 1-1/2" hem. Do not stitch.

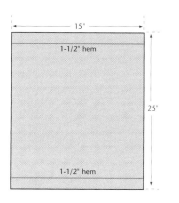

❶

15"

1-1/2" hem

25"

1-1/2" hem

2 Unfold the hem. Fold the rectangle in half widthwise and stitch sides with a 1/4" seam allowance. Turn right sides out.

3 Re-fold the hem and press. Topstitch the hem in place at the top and bottom of the hem.

4 To make the loops, cut three fabric strips from quilt fabric (two strips from heavy weight fabric like denim). With right sides together, stitch with a 1/4" seam allowance. (Note: Cut the fabric strips the length of the fabric for stability.)

5 On the short-stitched edge of the loop, insert a yardstick into the wrong side of the loop.

6 While holding onto the seam allowances, continue moving the loop onto the yardstick until the loop is completely turned to the right side. Pull the turned loop off the yardstick and press.

7 On the inside of the satchel, stitch the two loops onto the inside hem over previous stitching.

8 Press loops toward the top of the satchel and stitch a squared "X" as shown, for stability.

9 Sew a double row of stitching 1/4" apart down the center of the satchel through all layers. Mark the fabric where snaps are to be set. Attach snaps according to the manufacturer's instructions to the strap and satchel, using the correct components. Adjust measurements of the satchel according to the size of the walker or wheelchair. Add pockets for convenience before stitching the sides together. Add more caps and sockets to the loop for adjusting the length of straps for a walker or wheelchair.

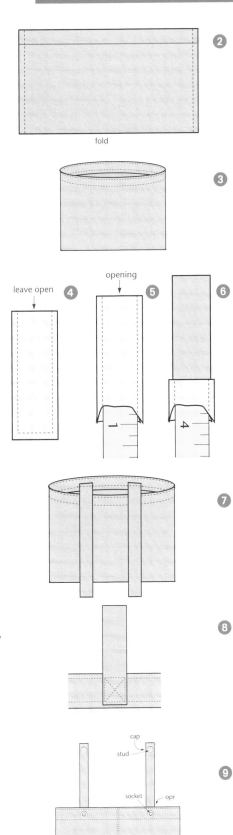

Tip:

For a wheelchair satchel, it may be helpful to secure the straps to both ends of the satchel.

Tip:

If you have a one-way fabric design, cut 4 rectangles 15" wide by 24-3/4" long. Be sure all fabrics are lying in the appropriate direction and stitch the two bottom sections of the satchel. Continue with the remaining instructions to complete the satchel.

Don't give up on a favorite outfit just because the snap is worn out or throw away a baby garment because the snap is missing. Get more life out of clothing—repair, replace, recycle!

Repair, Replace, Recycle

Repairing Worn Snaps

There are times when snaps fail to open and close properly—especially with prong-style snaps. In order to help the socket and stud close properly, here are some tips for socket tension adjustment.

❶ If the snap will not stay closed and keeps popping open during wear, simply use a small needle-nose pliers to slightly squeeze the socket segments tighter by moving the segments found on the inner ring of the socket, as shown. Keep in mind a little movement goes a long way. Tighten the segments only slightly.

❷ If the snap tension is too tight and the snap is tugging on the fabric, follow the above instructions except push the segments away from the center of the socket. Again, a little movement goes a long way.

If this method does not help the garment stay closed, you will have to remove the snap set and replace the snaps. (See page 143 and 144 for instructions on how to remove the snaps.) Attach new snaps according to manufacturer's instructions and use the same style snap components that were removed from the garment.

❶

To Tighten

❷

To Loosen

Clothing Repair

There may be times when a snap causes fabric to tear. If this happens, follow these fabric repair steps.

1 If the snap is still intact on the garment, use the snap removal techniques found on page 143 and 144. Identify the location where the snap pulled from the fabric.

2 On the right side of the fabric, pin a 1" square of stabilizer over the hole.

1

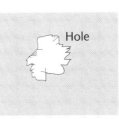

Hole

2

What You Will Need:

Stabilizer
  (embroidery
  tear-off type)
Fusible woven
  interfacing
Matching thread
Replacement snaps
Snap attaching tool
Fusible web and
  matching fabric
  (optional)
Sewing machine
  (optional)
Darning foot
  (optional)
Hand sewing needle
  (optional)

3 On the wrong side of the fabric, attach a 1" square of woven fusible interfacing over the hole. Or try attaching fusible web to a matching fabric for use as the interfacing to patch the hole. For polar-type fabrics, pin a 1" square of woven, non-fusible interfacing. Do not touch an iron to Polarfleece. It can melt the fibers.

4 Darn the area over the hole through all thicknesses on the right side of the garment using either a sewing machine or needle and thread. Be sure to stay within the confines of the diameter of the snap and catch all the fabric surrounding the hole.

5 Attach a new snap over the darned area making sure the snap top is larger than the stitched area.

6 Remove the tear-away stabilizer from the right side of the fabric.

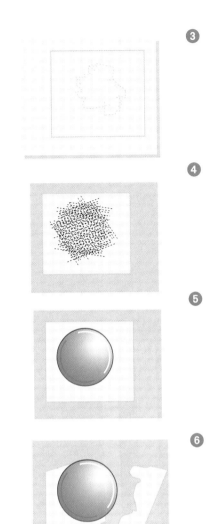

Snap Replacement

Replacing snaps due to misalignment, a style change or a missing snap is an easy task. The following are removal methods for the various snap styles.

Finding an exact snap match can be difficult and since snap components are not inter-changeable, be sure to remove all four parts of the snap when repairing ready-made garments. Identify the style of snap to be removed—post-style snaps will leave a hole in the fabric and prong-style snaps will leave teeth marks in the fabric.

When choosing a replacement snap, it may be necessary to comporomise on the replacement style of snap depending on snap availability. See page 24 for more information on snap styles.

See page 24

What You Will Need:

Snap Remover
  (See page 145)
Drill and drill bit set
Small head
  screwdriver
Replacement snap
  sets
Snap attaching tool
Wire cutters
Needle nose pliers

Post-Style Snap Removal

❶ To remove the socket and stud of a spring-ring snap, you will need a drill and an appropriately sized drill bit. To determine what size drill bit you need, look inside the socket or stud, and measure the post roll.

❷ Choose a drill bit that is slightly larger than the outside edge of the roll. Drill in the center of the post roll inside the socket until the socket begins to turn. Do not go all the way through the snap. Repeat this for the stud portion of the snap.

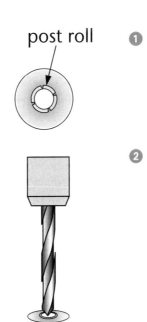

post roll ❶

❷

Parallel-Spring Snap Removal

Use the instructions on previous page for the spring-ring socket removal. For the stud, simply use a wire cutter to cut off the stud portion of the snap close to the flange. The stud and post will immediately separate.

Discard all the damaged snap components. Do not try to reuse the snap—it will not function properly.

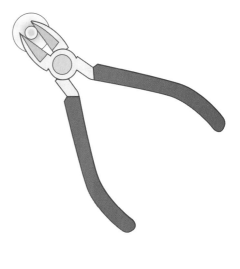

Prong-Style Snap Removal

There is more than one way to remove a prong-style snap. Gently insert a small, flat-headed screwdriver between the fabric and the socket or stud. Slowly and carefully twist the head of the screwdriver to loosen the snap component. Repeat this action clockwise around the socket or stud until the component unlocks from the prongs. Gently move the fabric away from the prongs. If the snap

leaves a hole in the fabric, patch the hole by using the instructions found on page 141. Another way is to create and use a Snap Remover that you can make yourself. Refer to page 146 for removing snaps with a Snap Remover.

Making a Snap Remover

If you remove snaps professionally or like to find good buys on children's clothing with missing snaps at garage sales or Mom-to-Mom Resale Events, then creating a quick and easy snap remover is for you! Here's what you'll need to do.

What You Will Need:

Electric Drill
7" Bent Trimmers
Sharpening Stone
1/8" Drill Bit
  designed to cut
  steel
Scrap Piece of
  Wood

1 To drill a hole into the 7" bent trimmers, load the special steel cutting drill bit into the drill. Open the trimmers, turn on the drill and close the trimmers one-third of the way from the tip onto the bit as illustrated.

2 When finished making the hole, open the trimmers and use a sharpening stone to remove the sharp edges. Be sure to dull the blade and the surrounding hole surface so the trimmers will no longer cut objects and does not have any sharp edges.

3 To remove prong-style snaps, gently squeeze the industrial snap remover under the lip of the socket or stud. Be sure to place your hand or a wash cloth over the component you are removing to prevent the snap from flying off the fabric. Discard all the snap components when removed from the garment. Do not try to reuse the snap—it will not function properly.

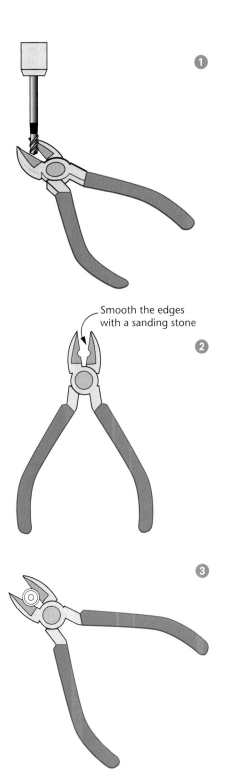

1

Smooth the edges with a sanding stone

2

3

Metal Sensitivity

For metal-sensitive individuals who like to wear snaps but can't because of an allergic reaction called nickel dermatitis they experience when the snap comes in contact with the skin, there is a simple remedy. On ready-to-wear garments where the snap already exists, simply fuse a square of tricot interfacing to the inside of the garment covering the snap where it touches the skin.

If you are constructing the garment or wish to remove the snaps from ready-to-wear garments, use snaps made from stainless steel. Check with your snap supplier for this special metal. Most stainless steel snaps are made with a dull finish and in most cases will not have a signature on the stud due to the lightweight nature of the metal.

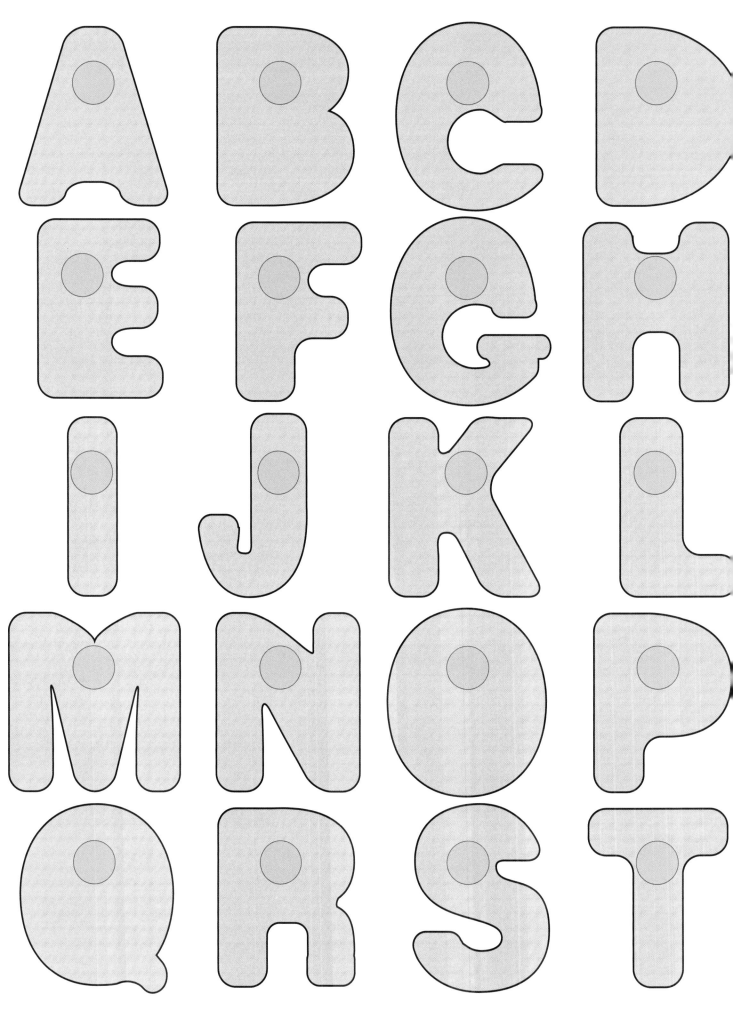

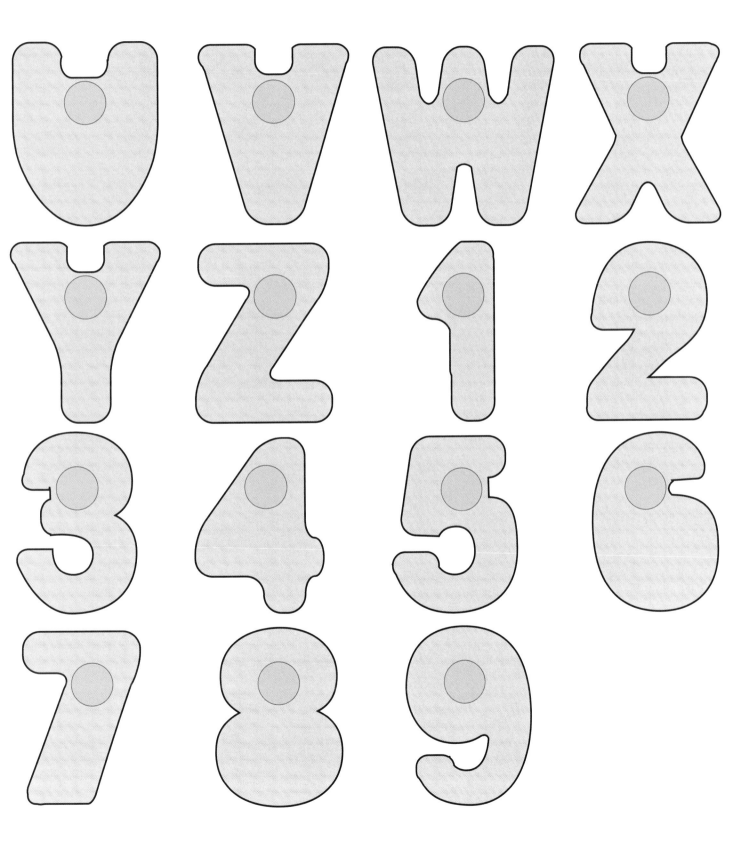

The products mentioned in this book are available at your local sewing notion retailer or through these dependable resources:

Cactus Punch
12995 N. Oracle Rd. #141-327
Dept. SB
Tucson, AZ 85739
(800)933-8081
www.cactus-punch.com
Over 1000 custom & original embroidery designs

Fasnap Corporation
23669 Reedy Dr., Dept. SB.
Elkhart, IN 46514
(800)624-2058
www.fasnap.com
Heavy-duty, marine and automotive snaps

Ghee's
2620 Centenary, #2-250
Dept. SB
Shreveport, LA 71104
www.ghees.com
Art-to-wear patterns and books; hardware and patterns for purses

HooVer Products
427 Grand Ave. #A
Dept. SB
San Jacinto, CA 92582
(909)654-4627
Pres-n-Snap - snap attaching tool

Kwik Sew Pattern Co.
Look for the Kwik Sew Patterns at your local fabric retailer or call 888-KWIK-SEW for a store nearest you.
www.kwiksew.com

Nancy's Notions
P.O. Box 683
Dept. SB
Beaver Dam, WI 53916
(800)833-0690
www.nancysnotions.com
Quality sewing notions by mail

Prym/Dritz Corporation
Look for the Prym/Dritz products at your local sewing notion retailer or call (800)845-4948 for a store nearest you.
www.dritz.com

Ready Bias-The Quilter's Binding
1747 Spyglass Lane
Dept. SB
Moraga, CA 94556
(888)873-2427
100% cotton, ready-to-use continuous binding in 40 solids and prints

SewBaby!
P.O. Box 11683, Dept. SB
Champaign, IL 61826
(800)249-1907
www.sewbaby.com
Fabrics, patterns, notions for children and adults—by mail

Scrubs-Buy-Mail
5737 Laguna Quail Way, Dept SB
Elk Grove, CA 95758
(800)332-1582
www.scrubs-buy-mail.com
Patterns and fabrics for scrubs

SJR Sew With Class
4109 E. Deer Hart Dr.
Dept. SB
Chillicothe, IL 61523
www.sewwithclass.com
Art-to-wear books and patterns

The Snap Source, Inc.
P.O. Box 99733
Dept. SB
Troy, MI 48099
(800)725-4600
www.snapsource.com
Look for The SnapSetter™ snap
attaching tool and long-prong
snaps at your local sewing, fabric
or quilting retailer

Time-Saver Tool Corporation
P.O. Box 4299, Dept. SB.
Hammond, IN 46324
(219)845-2500
Clinch-Fast-Kit snap attaching tools
and snaps

Vicar International
2424 Iorio St.
Dept. SB
Union, NJ 07083
Heavy-duty, marine and automo-
tive snaps

For more information about
connecting with the Home Sewing
Industry and others who share the
love of sewing, contact:

The Home Sewing Association
1350 Broadway
Suite 1601, Dept. SB
New York, NY 10018
www.sewing.org

The American Sewing Guild
9140 Ward Parkway
Dept. SB
Kansas City, MO 64114
www.asg.org

Index

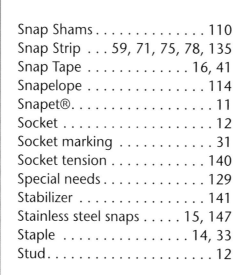

Jeanine Twigg is the founder and owner of The Snap Source, Inc., an international corporation specializing in a large selection of colored snaps and snap attaching tools. In 1991, as Jeanine was sewing for her two young children, she wondered why the snaps on the market weren't as durable as the snaps used on ready-to-wear garments. She discovered the answer, designed and patented a snap attaching tool, found the perfect snaps and is now sharing the secrets of setting snaps with sewing consumers around the world.

In addition, Jeanine travels across the United States teaching seminars on her favorite subjects—snaps, sewing for all ages and Polarfleece. She is on the board of directors for the Home Sewing Assocation—a non-profit organization dedicated to promoting the growth of the Home Sewing Industry. Her mission is to motivate and educate consumers in all aspects of sewing and to help keep the industry she loves thriving.

To contact Jeanine Twigg at the Snap Source, Inc., write to her at P.O. Box 99733, Troy, MI 48099. Be sure to ask for a catalog or inquire about her upcoming seminar schedule. Look for the Snap Source® products at a fabric, sewing or quilting store nearest you or call the Snap Source, Inc. at (800)725-4600 for more information.

DISCOVER ENDLESS PROJECTS AND ADD YOUR CREATIVE TOUCHES

SEW & GO BABY
A Collection of Practical Baby Gear Projects
by Jasmine Hubble
Sew & Go Baby presents 30 practical projects for you to assemble a memorable gift or party for the special baby or toddler in your life. Clear directions, easy-to-follow patterns and full-color photography will enable you to create an entire baby-shower, essential baby gear, clothes, accessories and thoughtful sibling gifts.

Softcover • 8-1/4 x 10-7/8 • 96 pages
300 Illustrations • 75 color photos
SFTB • $19.95

SEW THE ESSENTIAL WARDROBE FOR 18-INCH DOLLS
Complete Instructions & Full Size Patterns for 18 Modern Outfits
by Joan Hinds & Jean Becker
Dress your doll for any occasion-from a holiday party to a workout at the gym. Authors have designed 18 modern outfits for today's popular 18-inch dolls. Step-by-step instructions are illustrated with helpful diagrams, clear and easy-to-follow sewing instructions, and beautiful color photos for lots of inspiration. Full-size patterns are printed on two convenient pull-outs.

Softcover • 8-1/4 x 10-7/8 • 96 pages
250 Diagrams • 45 color photos
EWD • $19.95

ADVENTURES WITH POLAR-FLEECE
A Sewing Expedition
by Nancy Cornwell
Allow author Nancy Cornwell to lead you on a sewing expedition. Explore and discover endless project possibilities for the entire family. Sew a collection of fifteen projects for play, work, fashion, comfort and warmth. The heart of a fallen-away sewer will soon be recaptured and new sewers will be intrigued and inspired.

Softcover • 8-1/2 x 11 • 160 pages
150 Illustrations • 200 photographs
AWPF • $19.95

MORE RIBBON EMBROIDERY BY MACHINE
by Marie Duncan & Betty Farrell
Nineteen exciting projects using the popular ribbon embroidery by machine decorating method. Baby wearables to elegant evening bags are detailed in this instructional volume. Includes how to embellish ready-made items as well as techniques for incorporating beading and heirloom sewing. Sound advice for beginner and expert alike.

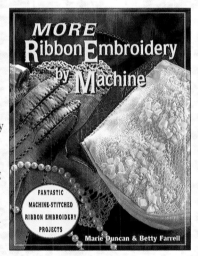

Softcover • 8-1/4 x 10-7/8 • 96 pages
100 color photos
BCUR • $21.95

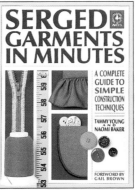
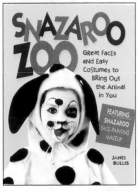